The First New Zealanders

By the same author:
THE SHADOW OF THE LAND: a novel
LAND FROM THE MASTHEAD
HIDDEN WATER

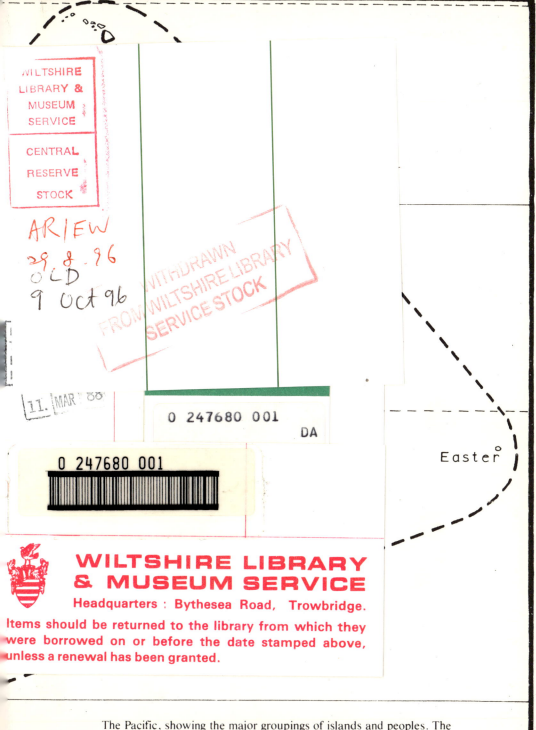

Easter

The Pacific, showing the major groupings of islands and peoples. The
inset of New Zealand shows archaeological sites mentioned in the text.

The First
New Zealanders

Philip Houghton

HODDER & STOUGHTON
AUCKLAND   LONDON   SYDNEY

To my mother
and in memory of my father

Contents

Acknowledgments

Most importantly I owe thanks to the Maori groups and communities who have approved of these studies. Without their goodwill in this most sensitive field there would have been no hope of progress. They have in turn educated me on matters relevant to being a New Zealander. I have a particular debt here to Muru Walters for discussion and direction.

Many others have assisted in various ways with the studies on which much of this book is based. I am grateful to K. J. Dennison for much meticulous laboratory analysis; B. M. and M. de Lambert, whose facilities, expertise and interest have made the X-ray studies possible; P. de Souza for lucid statistical advice and some original ideas; M. R. Kean for many critical discussions and a nice balance of scepticism and encouragement; B. F. Leach for ever-available advice and unflagging enthusiasm; and W. D. Trotter and the University of Otago for encouragement and support.

Others have helped at times, and inevitably names will be missed — to these my apologies. I thank M. Buranarugsa, A. D. Campbell, J. M. Davidson, the late Dr R. Duff, J. F. Gwynne, C. F. W. Higham, H. M. Leach, G. M. Mason, B. McFadgen, S. G. Park, M. A. L. Phillipps, R. J. Scarlett, A. I. F. Simpson, D. G. Sutton, M. M. Trotter.

J. B. Carman, J. M. Davidson, R. C. Green, M. R. Kean, B. F. Leach, W. D. Trotter and M. Walters have read, corrected and improved the manuscript, but of course cannot be blamed for its deficiencies.

M. E. Ogilvie, who prepared a number of diagrams, and A. Barnes, S. K. Murphy, M. Owens and M. E. Scoular, who typed the manuscript, have made my task much easier by their pleasantness and efficiency.

1. Introduction

Some eighty million years ago, before the age of mammals, a fragment broke off Gondwanaland and drifted eastward. Subsequent major earth movements subtracted from it, added to it, until in quite recent geological time, no more than three or four million years ago, a recognisable New Zealand formed. It lacked the marsupials of its nearest neighbour, and any mammals except for a couple of species of bat. In protecting isolation the animal life went its own way. Flightless birds evolved, reaching their most striking form in the giant moa, *Dinornus maximus,* standing up to twelve feet tall. The tuatara survived, representative of a family of reptiles that elsewhere became extinct some sixty million years ago. Sea and wind allowed a greater interchange of plant life, yet this also developed its own very distinctive pattern, including a noticeable richness of ferns. And this same isolation hid it from man. New Zealand was the last substantial area of land to be reached by *Homo sapiens.* Intelligent precursors of man were shaping tools in Africa as New Zealand assumed much its present form, and modern man had been in Australia for some forty thousand years, and in the Americas for perhaps as long, before the first canoe ran up a New Zealand beach. Yet the history of these first New Zealanders is no less fascinating for being relatively recent — only yesterday, as it were, in the human story.

This is an account of only one aspect of that history — of the physical appearance, the state of health and the diseases of the inhabitants of prehistoric New Zealand, as interpreted from a study of physical remains. In places, where information from tradition or archaeology or linguistics has been required to create a fuller picture, I have tried to absorb and interpret the views of those knowledgeable in such fields, but of course all errors, misinterpretations and fixed ideas are my own.

For two centuries the Polynesians have aroused interest and become the subject of libraries of writings in a Eurocentric world. In part this has been because the European saw physical similarities between himself and the Polynesian, which was comforting when he found himself bested in trade, diplomacy or war. The romance of the Polynesian settlement of the furthest islands of the Pacific has given rise to a great number of works dealing with the Polynesian story as evidenced by tradition and custom, by the material things such as canoes and houses, adzes and fish hooks, and by the pattern of their languages; the story of a remarkable people in their vast ocean world. What is largely absent from most scientific accounts of the Polynesian past is anything much about the people themselves — as if all these other things could be modified, sometimes uniquely, over millennia, but the people themselves, the creators, at the very core, were unremarkable *Homo sapiens*.

The reality is different, as these pages try to show. And although particularly about the New Zealanders, the story has a wider relevance to all Polynesia and parts beyond. For example, the physical form of the first New Zealanders closely resembles that of other prehistoric Polynesians, and the physical similarities and differences within and beyond Polynesia are invaluable in tracing origins, movements and relationships across the Pacific. Again, the pattern of physical existence, however modified by environment and social custom, has basic similarities to the existence of tribal man anywhere.

One major reason why people figure less prominently than such things as carvings or adzes in accounts of New Zealand's past is clear. It is not possible to study human skeletal material in New Zealand, and indeed throughout Polynesia, without becoming aware that one is dealing with things of the deepest import to traditional belief, where the past and all relating to it is one with, and indivisible from, the present. Land and ancestors are all-pervading and all-important, and this book is about ancestors. To some, such studies and this account of what has been learned from them will be anathema; to others it will cause at least some disquiet. However, there are points to be considered.

Human skeletal material will continue to be frequently uncovered by natural erosion, by construction works of various kinds and, least often, by archaeological excavations. The latter can now only be legally undertaken in New Zealand with the authority of the Historic Places Trust, who are bound to consult with groups and communities who have a connection with the site. From this it follows that when skeletal material is uncovered its existence has usually been unsuspected and its relationship to modern groups is obscure. When such unknown remains are uncovered it is necessary on legal grounds alone to determine to whom and to what period they belong. Only a proper scientific examination can determine this.

It is inevitable then that human remains from the past will continue to be uncovered, and perforce will be scientifically examined. From such examination flows a great deal of information about the past, as well as some that is directly relevant to contemporary health problems amongst Maoris and Polynesians. This information is now of considerable interest to the many New

Zealanders with a wish to learn of the past of this country. The majority of these, not brought up against a traditional Maori background, find it hard to understand that the fruits of scientific study of New Zealand's past are considered by some to be largely irrelevant. It has been made clear to me that it is on the *marae*, in the ceremony, in the speeches with their references and allusions to the land and to the past, that the vital story, the real history, is set out. On the other hand, over the past few years I have communicated the results of various studies to local Maori groups. The interest and appreciation with which these have been received leads me to believe that a general account of this aspect of New Zealand's past does have its place. I am very much aware of the range and depth of feeling on these matters. With respect, I offer a version of the past based on a certain line of scientific evidence.

These studies are far from complete. A few matters, such as some aspects of physique, have been looked at fairly thoroughly. But all too often, comments and suggestions are based on inadequate material or an inadequate study of the material. Nevertheless they are offered here because, in their context, they do present a more realistic picture than some in common currency. In places I have tried to present complex biological situations in simple yet not oversimplified terms. For ease of reading I have avoided any footnotes in the text, as these are disconcerting to those not used to them. As compensation, a bibliography is appended. I tend not to use the name Maori, but rather New Zealander, or New Zealand Polynesian, or just Polynesian. There are several reasons for this. In the first place, the term Maori dates only from about the middle of the last century and was not used in prehistory by the New Zealanders as an overall description of themselves. Removed from the rest of the world, they had no necessity to see themselves as one people. Secondly, in the present context it tends to obscure the possibility of differences within New Zealand and the related possibility of multiple settlement. And the recurring term, Polynesian, stresses the Pacific origins and relationships.

Prehistory is defined as that period prior to continuous written records, and in New Zealand is generally taken to conclude with Cook's first visit in 1769. In determining what prehistoric New Zealanders were like, at least in the later prehistoric period, it is reasonable to draw — as I have frequently here — on the comments of early European visitors as well as on the information obtained from the physical remains.

2. The Archaeological Evidence

Skeletal remains may seem to be as inert and unchanging as the rocks around, but nothing could be further from the truth. The bone of which they are composed has been living material, and the evidence of the form and pattern of life remains in its structure. Bone forms the firm basis for body activity, the framework on which the muscles hang, yet it is also a very active tissue in the metabolic sense — that is, in the way biochemical reactions and changes are proceeding within it all the time and involving bone in the general functioning of the body. The minerals in it are far from fixed but are being replaced and renewed continually, as the bone substance itself is remodelled and altered by the cells in response to changing environment and activity. Particularly, bone forms the great body reserve of calcium which is important in many body functions, such as the clotting of blood and the normal working of the nerves. Other elements, 'trace' elements, are stored in bone, and not all their functions in the healthy body are yet clear. Bone may also take up undesirable elements from the environment. For example the element strontium is readily fixed in the molecular structure of bone, having passed through the food chain from its source in plants — milk is one dietary source of our strontium. Radioactive strontium from atomic explosions now exists in varying amounts in all mankind. Again, lead is an element lacking in prehistoric bone, but it is present in appreciable amounts in much modern bone as a result of the breathing of traces of exhaust gases from vehicles that use petrol treated with lead. In smaller amounts these 'unnatural' elements may be tolerated, but higher levels in bone would suggest an excessive amount in the whole body with various unhappy consequences.

At a grosser level, bone is not even the inert, rigid framework it appears, something to which the muscles and other soft tissues must mould themselves. Rather the situation is the other way round — bone is influenced by the soft tissues, responds to this influence, and moulds and changes according to the demands made on it. The story of these past demands, past patterns of living, can be read.

So the appearance of permanence to bone is something of an illusion. It has been living tissue and can survive to tell a great deal about the person to whom it belonged. When examined by various techniques this evidence can be obtained, and to understand how the techniques may be applied some idea of the finer structure of bone is required.

Bone consists of about one-third organic matter and two-thirds inorganic matter. The organic part is largely made up of strong fibres of a substance called collagen, the same that forms the basis of tendons and sinews and which collectively have a white, rather glistening appearance, in the fresh state. Single collagen fibres can only be seen microscopically, and under high magnification are seen to have a banded appearance, the bands being arranged at very regular intervals (*Fig. 2.1*). In bone the fibres are closely packed together, parallel to one another, in layers. The different layers have their fibres running in different directions. Distributed through this organic framework of collagen fibres are bone cells and blood vessels. Bone has quite a rich blood supply, further proof that it is an active tissue, changing with body needs. If it were as dead in life as it appears in the ground it would not need such a blood supply.

Fig. 2.1: *A microscopic view of collagen fibres magnified 20,000 times. In bone they are more closely packed than shown here, with the fibres in each layer parallel.*

As we shall see in a moment, there is a somewhat differing arrangement of these various organic components — collagen, bone cells and blood vessels — in different parts of a bone.

The inorganic component of bone is predominately a complex calcium phosphate compound called hydroxyapatite, or more simply, apatite. This material is deposited as needle-like crystals on the surface of the collagen fibres and the effect of this intimate association of organic and inorganic components in bone is to change quite considerably their individual properties. The change is analogous to the properties of concrete and steel as individual substances, and the difference that ensues when they are combined as ferrocement. Like cement, apatite is well adapted to resisting crushing forces, or compressive forces, but is poor at resisting disrupting, or what are termed tensile forces. The collagen fibres of bone, on the other hand, like the steel rods in ferrocement, are particularly well adapted to resisting tensile or disrupting forces, though they have poor resistance to crushing forces. In bone, where the inorganic and organic components are intimately combined, the resulting structure has greatly enhanced resistance to both compressive and tensile forces, just as does ferrocement compared with its individual components. An example of the crushing forces the bone has to resist is the body weight and any extra loads carried, while one of the tensile forces is that of the various muscles pulling on their attachments to the bone, though this is a very artificial sort of distinction as any force acting on a bone will cause tension in some parts and compression in others.

Bone is conveniently divided into two types, compact and spongy. A section down one of the long bones of the arm or leg (*Fig. 2.2*) shows the two types — compact bone is seen in the shaft, while spongy bone is found at the ends. As the name suggests, compact bone is dense and *Fig. 2.3* shows the typical appearance of human compact bone when seen under the microscope. The basis of its architecture is the osteon. This consists of a central canal, carrying small blood vessels, surrounded by concentric layers of collagen fibres. Within each layer most fibres run in the same direction, but from layer to layer the direction is different. In small holes in and between the layers are locked the bone cells. Compact bone is made up of several millions of such osteons, closely packed together.

Fig. 2.2: *A section of a longbone – in this figure, the tibia (lower leg) – shows the dense cortical bone along the shaft, and the spongy bone at each end. The marrow cavity lies in the shaft.*

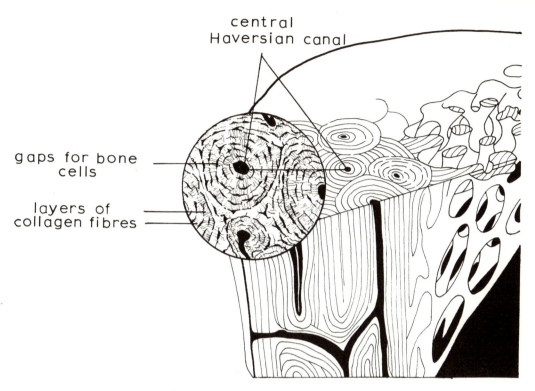

central
Haversian canal

gaps for bone
cells

layers of
collagen fibres

Fig. 2.3: *A section of a longbone near one end, with compact bone on the left and bands of spongy bone on the right. The inset shows the architecture of compact bone – an aggregation of osteons.*

By contrast, spongy bone lacks this regular appearance of osteons. To the naked eye it shows a meshwork of interlacing bands of bone called trabeculae, which are aligned according to the forces acting on the bone. Individual trabecula consist generally of layers of parallel packed collagen fibres with bone cells amongst them. Spongy bone has a better blood supply than compact bone and heals more readily if broken.

This picture of human bone is much simplified. As I've tried to stress, bone is a living tissue, changing with the demands made on it, and with age. For example, in younger people the outer layers of cortical bone are circumferential, like tree rings. With age these outer layers disappear, and are replaced by osteons, which become more numerous and smaller throughout the bone. Changes such as these may be of great value when ageing human remains from prehistory. The human pattern is also different from animal patterns when viewed under the microscope and it is

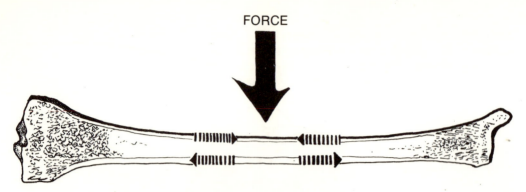

FORCE

Fig. 2.4: *The bending of the shaft of a long bone creates a compressive force on the nearside and a disruptive force on the opposite side. Between, the forces effectively cancel out, and no bone is needed for strength.*

possible sometimes to identify the source of the bone even from very small fragments.

Returning to the human condition: it can be seen from *Fig. 2.2* that the shaft of a long bone is hollow, this hollow being the marrow cavity. While such a cavity obviously lightens the bone, an advantage for any animal living on land, does it not weaken the bone? The answer lies in a consideration of the compressive and tensile forces acting on it. Consider a force applied to one side of a long bone (*Fig. 2.4*). The side on which the force is applied is exposed to a compressive or crushing force. The opposite side is exposed to a tensile or disrupting force. Between, there is an area where the forces cancel out, where there is a balance between compression and disruption. In this area no bone is required for there is no effective force to resist and a cavity can be formed to lighten the bone. It is only convenient, and secondary, that bone marrow should be found here.

We shall continually refer back to this basic structure of bone when talking about different aspects of these prehistoric studies, but the essential point is that bone (and the teeth should be included here too) differs from most other material in the human record of the past — the artefacts, the carvings and buildings and creations of man — in that it contains intimate evidence of the individual's growth and daily existence. We have to search out this evidence and there is no doubt that bone is frustrating material to work with. For example we may be able to reliably comment on the number of illnesses someone suffered in child-hood, the amount of meat eaten, and the number of children a woman bore: but we can only uncommonly give the precise cause of death of a person, for most afflictions immediately leading to death leave no imprint on the bone — as far as we can determine at present. One adds this, because bone is the focus of an immense amount of medical and scientific research throughout the world, and new methods of analysis, directly or indirectly applicable to these studies of prehistoric man, are continually emerging.

Incidentally, this emphasis on bone as a living material applies also to the piles of shell, fish bone, bird bone and other animal remains — the rubbish heaps of prehistory — that make up the middens that pepper this country from one end to the other. These too have been living, and scientific analysis of these unprepossessing piles is similarly rewarding. From them the diet of the inhabitants of an area can be determined, together with any change between the seasons and over the years. Change in climate and landscape can be judged and the growing scarcity and eventual extinction of a species noted. It is difficult to convince people that a midden heap can be an exciting thing. The news that crates and crates of material have been removed from an archaeological site usually calls up the rumour that large amounts of carvings and greenstone and even human bones are being carted away. The reality of shells, animal bone, soil samples, charcoal and oven stones is more prosaic to the uninitiated eye, but it can be more rewarding in the unravelling of the story of the past than glamorous artefacts of greenstone.

Table 2.1 lists the sort of information that can be derived from skeletal material. It can be seen that a fairly detailed picture of the life of an individual can be built up, and where several are involved a broader picture of their existence as a community can be established. No isolated bone can be dismissed as being inconsequential, as offering no useful information, for a single long bone can provide much of the information contained in the entire skeleton.

Of the various procedures and techniques of analysis of bone, some of the most basic are the methods of estimating the time that has elapsed since death. How long ago did this person die? The ideal method of determination would be non-destructive of material and would give a precise and accurate date for the record. Life is never as simple as that, unfortunately, and errors and hazards abound. Within the time-span of prehistoric human settlement of New Zealand — at present considered to be about a thousand years — the usual method of dating various forms of once-living material is by carbon-14 estimation. It is based on the principle that carbon in the environment exists in a number of forms or isotopes, namely, carbon-12, carbon-13, and the naturally-occurring radioactive isotope, carbon-14. During life the organism or plant takes up these isotopes in definite proportions, and with death such uptake ceases. After death the radioactive carbon-14 continues to decay to carbon-12. If we know the rate of decay of this carbon-14 — and it is known — then the time elapsed since death can be determined by measuring the amount of carbon-14 in the organism or plant. In bone, it is the carbon-14 content of the organic, collagen fraction of the bone that is nowadays determined. It should be stressed that there remain many problems and sources of errors with this technique. For example, while the rate of decay of carbon-14 is fixed, the amount naturally present in the atmosphere has varied over time. Again, recent organic material such as soil humus may contaminate the specimen, making it appear younger than it is. In addition carbon-14 dating has the disadvantage, when dealing with skeletal material, of at present requiring quite a large amount of bone. For a skeleton buried about a thousand years ago in New Zealand the analysis may indeed require just about all the surviving bone. The method is destructive and this is not really acceptable for old and valuable material. Also, local feeling which might be favourable towards a scientific examination of remains would justifiably look askance at such wholesale destruction just to obtain a date. The promise does exist of refinements of the carbon-14 method, requiring only minute amounts of material, but at present these are not available. Radio-carbon dating is also expensive in time and equipment. It is a very sophisticated form of analysis.

Other possible ways of dating bone are by determination of its fluorine content, or its nitrogen content. These are generally described as relative dating methods — that is, they are considered useful in determining which are the older and which are the more recent specimens from a single site or excavation; but because of the many variable factors involved, such as soil acidity, temperature, and exposure to water, they are not generally considered to give either a specific date in the past, or to allow comparison between sites in different parts of a country, or different parts of the world.

While they are both labelled 'relative' dating techniques their basis is very different. Nitrogen levels are an expression of the amount of collagen remaining in the bone — that is, of the amount of organic material remaining, as nearly all the organic material is contained in the collagen. Nitrogen values will therefore decline with the age of the specimens. Fluoride levels, on the other hand, rise with age, by a process of trapping of fluoride ions in the mineral apatite structure. If the bone is buried in soil rich in fluoride or exposed to water rich in fluoride, then the rise may be very great.

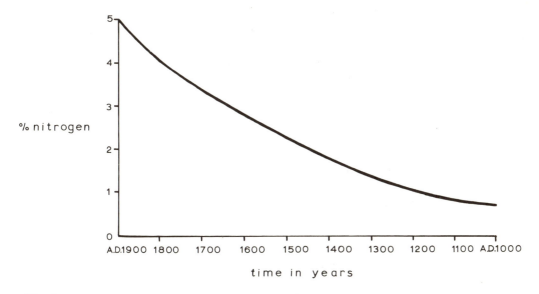

Fig. 2.5: *Graph showing the decline in nitrogen in buried bone under New Zealand coastal conditions.*

A further practical difference is that fluoride estimation is rather complex and tedious, whereas nitrogen estimation is relatively simple, and is economical of bone. It is possible to accurately determine the nitrogen level of a bone sample with no more material than would cover a thumbnail. Furthermore, in the New Zealand situation, where we appear to be dealing with a settlement period of only some one thousand years, fluorine has usually not risen to significant levels, and nitrogen, fortunately, has not yet sunk to insignificant values.

The estimation of the nitrogen level of the bone therefore looks to be particularly useful for the New Zealand situations, and what has been found is that its use can be extended beyond a single site. On a world-wide basis nitrogen levels certainly have little relevance to absolute dates in time. But within a limited, reasonably-consistent environment — and for this purpose coastal New Zealand, from whence comes most material, over the past one thousand years seems to be such an environment — the rate of decay of collagen in the bone seems to be fairly constant, and dependent more on time than any variability in soil acidity, temperature and so on. By the standards of, say the Ethiopian desert, New Zealand soils are not kind to bone, but the rate of degradation throughout the country seems fairly similar.

Here on average, over a thousand years the nitrogen content of a human bone will fall from about 5 percent to 1 percent (*Fig. 2.5*). By contrast, the bone sample from the Ethiopian desert might still after a thousand years have a nitrogen level of 4 percent.

These New Zealand values are only provisional and may have to be modified as results accumulate. But until some other cheap yet accurate dating method emerges, nitrogen levels will probably continue to prove a useful guide to bone age in New Zealand. We have yet to encounter a situation where the age of bone as estimated by its nitrogen content is distinctly and grossly at odds with all other evidence. There are one or two situations where it disagrees with the carbon-14 date, but where other evidence suggests that the nitrogen date is more likely to be correct.

When bone has been exposed to fire, the degradation of nitrogen has been artificially hastened and the nitrogen level is no longer useful.

This use of the nitrogen level of the bone allows us to place a great deal of skeletal material in some sort of time context, and as soon as this is done information tumbles out — we can see and interpret changes over time in some aspects of prehistoric existence that were hidden before because there was no time depth for the material.

The nitrogen content of bone gives an idea of the amount of collagen — of organic matter — remaining in it. It is possible to look at this breakdown of collagen in a different way. Collagen is a protein made up of a number of components called amino acids. It has been claimed that these degrade at different rates with time and if this was so an analysis of the amino acids remaining in a bone specimen might turn out to be useful in determining its age. In point of fact, when we came to look at the various amino acids in bone we found that their rates of degradation were similar and that no advantage was gained by an expensive and tedious amino acid analysis as opposed to a simple estimation of the nitrogen level.

These aspects of bone analysis and dating had one of their earliest and most famous applications in the exposure of the Piltdown forgery. For forty years Piltdown Man, *Eoanthropus dawsonii* — Dawn Man — was the British reply to the Neandertals, of which the French seemed to have an unreasonable monopoly. International rivalry does seem to have been one of the factors contributing to the success of the deception. In the discussion following the original presentation of the specimens at the Royal Geological Society meeting on 18 December, 1912, it is recorded:

Prof. A. Keith regarded the discovery of fossil human remains just announced as by far the most important ever made in England, and of equal, if not of greater consequence than any other discovery yet made, either at home or abroad . . . In the speaker's opinion, Tertiary man had thus been discovered in Sussex.

Even at the meeting there was a dissenting voice. One Professor Waterston pointed out that "if the reconstruction of the cranium and mandible were accepted, it was quite clear that the former was human in practically all its essential characters; while the latter with equal clearness resembled in all its details, the mandible of the chimpanzee. It was, therefore, very difficult to believe that the two specimens could have come from the same individual."

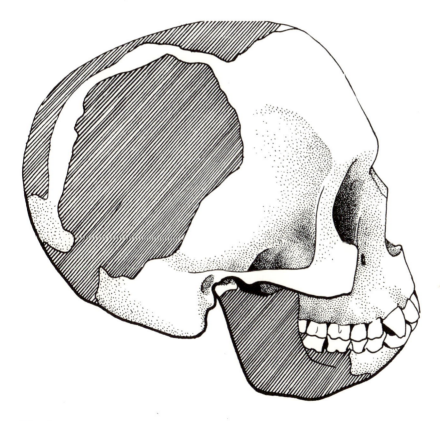

Fig. 2.6: *Dawn Man. A bad case of nationalistic blindness. Note the convenient absence of the condyle, where mandible joins the cranium. (The fragments found are cross-hatched, the remainder is reconstruction.)*

But the loyalists won — after all, as Dr Smith Woodward pointed out: "The swamps and forests of the Weald in early Pleistocene times may have been a refuge for a backward race." For forty years Dawn Man held a place in the evolutionary texts, with his troubling association of jaw and cranium — and the former so inconveniently, or conveniently, broken just before the place of attachment to the cranium (*Fig. 2.6*). There were always sceptics, such as the great biologist Weidenreich, or the New Zealand dentist and anthropologist R. M. S. Taylor who pointed out that the wear on the teeth could not be natural and that the canine was misidentified. Such news from the colonies was very bad, and ignored. But at last the qualms grew too great and a fluorine analysis was carried out on cranium and jaw. The jaw gave values typical of modern bone while the cranium appeared somewhat older. Nitrogen estimates gave a similar picture. It appeared that not only could the two parts not belong together, but far from being in the order of one hundred thousand years old, they were of recent origin. The cranium was human and the jaw possibly of a Sarawak baboon.

Since those days techniques have been improved and simplified, and such chemical analysis of bone is routine in skeletal studies. Presumably it would be difficult to get away with a Piltdown-type forgery today.

There are other indirect but often useful methods of dating excavated material, and some of these are set out in Table 2.2. There may be artefacts — adzes, fish hooks, and so on — known to belong to a particular period of prehistory. Artefacts made of the volcanic glass, obsidian, used for cutting tools, are particularly useful for dating purposes. Different obsidians have the curious property of absorbing water at given rates, which can be determined experimentally. Such absorption starts anew from a freshly exposed surface, and the depth of hydration into the stone can be observed in a section under the microscope. Thus the time that elapsed since the artefact was made can be judged.

The stratigraphy of the site — that is, the layers of soil — may prove a guide to age, when it is known from geological evidence when a certain layer was formed. For example, ash showers from Rangitoto in the Waitemata harbour occurred during an eruption dated to about AD 1350 and this provides a guide when dating excavations on the adjacent areas of Auckland. Wood obtained from a site may be dated by comparing its annual ring pattern with that of similar trees of known age. This will indicate the period during which the tree grew, and died, if not necessarily the time when it was utilised by man, which could possibly have occurred years after the death of the tree.

All these additional methods are at times useful, and they assist in calibrating the simple and direct estimation of the nitrogen level in the bone. For without dates, without some sense of time, prehistory is just a dark confusion, without pattern or coherence. As soon as we can place people in it the light starts to grow.

Table 2.1

The information that may be gained from the analysis of skeletal material

1 Age of the individual at death.
2 Sex of adults.
3 Stature (height) and body proportions.
4 Some details of the type of diet, and its adequacy.
5 The pattern of regular physical activity.
6 The general state of health, both in past years (as a child) and in adult life.
7 Specific diseases suffered.
8 The cause of death (sometimes).
9 The number of children borne by the women.
10 Relationships between individuals within a group, and between groups. This gives information on trade routes, migration and so on.
11 The time that has elapsed since death.
12 The collation of information on individuals allows overall comments to be made on population size, population changes, etc.
13 Some aspects of physique and health are relevant to understanding health problems today.
14 Knowledge of medicine and surgery possessed by prehistoric people from evidence of treatment on the individual.
15 Cultural practices associated with the human body, such as head-shaping, or trephination.
Note: When skeletal material is examined in place by experts the information obtained is likely to be more substantial. Material in the laboratory can tell a story, but if it is examined in context as well the story is much fuller.

Table 2.2

Methods of dating prehistoric material

METHOD	*COMMENTS*
Direct	
Nitrogen	Easily performed on small amount of bone. Useful rough guide to age of material. Measures the amount of organic material left in the bone. The rate of degradation of this is probably similar throughout New Zealand, but the values cannot be compared with other environments.
Fluorine	More difficult to perform than nitrogen. Indicates the amount of fluorine added to the mineral component of the bone, which is very dependent on the local environment. Not useful for human material in New Zealand.
Carbon-14	Invaluable for estimating time since death, and results are comparable world-wide. Measures the amount of radioactive carbon left in the bone. Requires quite a lot of bone (50-300 grams), sophisticated equipment, and is open to certain errors.
Indirect	
Artefacts	These may be known to belong to a particular prehistoric period.
Obsidian	Artefacts made of this volcanic glass absorb water at a constant rate at their newly-flaked surfaces. The depth of hydration can be observed under a microscope and the time since manufacture judged.
Stratigraphic	Certain soil layers, such as those formed by volcanic ash showers of known date, may allow an excavation to be dated.
Tree rings	Wooden material from an excavation may be dated by comparing the annual rings with a known, dated pattern of rings.

3. Physique

"The Natives of this Country are a strong, raw-boned, well made, Active People, rather above than under the common size, especially the Men." This is Cook's comment in the journal of the first voyage. Sir Joseph Banks noted: "The men are of the size of the larger Europeans, stout, clean-limbed and active." Augustus Earle, observing "with the critical eye of the artist", noted them to be "generally taller and larger men than Europeans." The Frenchman du Clesmeur, of the expedition led by the unfortunate Marion du Fresne, wrote: "The New Zealanders are generally tall and well made." The recurring observation by early European visitors was that the New Zealanders were, by European standards, tall and robust.

Such statements have to be considered in the context of their time. There is abundant evidence, particularly from the physical records of conscripts into the various armies, that European stature has increased greatly over the past two centuries. (This is largely a result of the general improvement in diet and living conditions in these countries.) For example, the average height of Frenchmen and Dutchmen has risen by nearly six inches in one hundred and fifty years, from about five foot two inches to more than five foot seven inches. Such a statement might arouse disbelief — the change appears just too dramatic — but there is cast-iron evidence from an even earlier period in the shape of suits of armour. These indicate that most of the medieval knights were a stunted five foot three inches or thereabouts. Again, a study of the hammock space on Nelson's flagship *Victory* and the height below decks leads to the conclusion that no matter how harsh shipboard life was, men just must have been smaller in those days in Europe.

Cook's observation that the New Zealanders were of rather more than average European stature must not therefore be read by modern standards (though Cook himself is said to have stood close to six feet tall). Bank's comment on the 'size of the larger Europeans' can be taken to refer to the size of the better-nourished upper class to which he belonged. Other observers gave specific estimates for the Polynesian. The surgeon John Savage in 1814 noted: "The men are usually from five foot eight inches to six feet in height; well-proportioned . . . ." Lieutenant Roux of Marion du Fresne's ship commented: "These islanders are generally of tall stature, well proportioned . . . Some, who appeared to be tallest amongst them, and whom we measured, were all over six feet in height . . ."

It is also relevant that another adjective frequently used in these physical descriptions of the New Zealander is 'stout'. While this did not, two hundred years ago, have the same suggestion of fatness or overweight that it does today, it did indicate a strongly-built, well-fleshed people. This was not a race to whom thinness lent an illusion of height.

The first substantial record of physical measurements on the Maori was made by A. S. Thomson, surgeon of the 58th Regiment, in 1849. He wrote: ". . . I recorded the height of 147 men, above the age of puberty, who presented themselves at the military hospital in Auckland in April, 1849, for Vaccination, the measurements being all taken without shoes or stockings . . . The average height of these 147 New Zealanders was 5ft 6¾in. The average of 80 students of the University of Cambridge, between 18 and 20 years of age, was 5ft 9¼in., and that of upwards of 800 students in the University of Edinburgh . . . was 5ft 8⁷/₁₀in., but from both of these an inch should be deducted for the shoes. The average height of 900 Belgians . . . from the Government Register, was 5ft 4¾in."

Thomson's university students would undoubtedly have been drawn from the better fed and housed proportion of the population of the British Isles, and his blanket reduction of height by a mere inch to allow for shoes seems inadequate. The Belgian figure looks more convincingly like a national sample. In addition his Maori sample sounds to have been far from mature, the criterion merely being that they had reached the age of puberty. If we take this as being any age from fourteen years onward, his sample was likely to have had a lot of growth left in it, particularly as in the Polynesian there is significant growth in height in the spine in the third decade — a point we will return to.

The major study on the stature of a group reasonably close to being full-blooded Maori is the extensive series of measurements made by Peter Buck on the Maori Battalion returning from the First World War. Of the 814 men over twenty years of age, 424 classed themselves as full-blooded Maoris. While for reasons of pride some may have denied any Pakeha ancestry, there can now be no improvement on this as a Maori sample. The returning Battalion contained a number of men of lesser physical build who had been enlisted to maintain the numerical strength of the Battalion in the face of the great loss of life from injury and disease. Buck therefore judged this group to be a fair representation of Maori males, with, if anything, a bias towards those of lesser physique.

He obtained an average height for these 424 men of five feet seven inches. This is remarkably close to Thomson's figure and in agreement with the early observations of the New Zealanders as a tall race; for even today an average height of five foot seven inches is considered, on a world-wide basis, to indicate a tall group. And for Buck's men the effect of some hundred years of changing environment and disease patterns must be considered. The First World War occurred not long after the nadir of Maori health and population, when the extinction of the race was often predicted. In general these men are most unlikely to have had the benefit in their early years of the best diet, housing, and health care, and any environmental influence on their stature is more likely to have been unfavourable than favourable, to have reduced it rather than increased it.

There is therefore plenty of support from historical records and actual measurement for the suggestion that the early contact New Zealanders, before European genes and disease were rife, were a tall people, averaging perhaps five foot eight inches in height, with men of six feet being fairly common. The question is, how does the skeletal record support this estimate — or, for that matter, how can one possibly determine a prehistoric individual's height?

It has been known for many years that there is a high correlation between the lengths of the long bones of the arm or leg of an individual, and his height. By studying a large group of people it is possible to develop equations which relate the length of any given bone, or selection of bones, to height. A simple example of such an equation is

$$\text{Stature} = 70.45 + (3.08 \times \text{length of humerus})$$

In general, the more long bones of an individual that are measured, the more accurate will be the height estimate, and the leg bones give more accurate results than do the arm bones because the former are actual components of the height.

However, the races of man are not built all to the same proportions. Leonardo's famous drawing of the proportions of man divides stature equally between the lower limb and the axial length (trunk and head). That is, a circle with centre at the pubis touches the top of the head and the soles of the feet (*Fig. 3.1*). Now this may have represented the ideal Florentine of the fifteenth century (Leonardo was actually illustrating here some principles enunciated centuries earlier by the Roman architect Vitruvius, and a quotation from Vitruvius is written in Leonardo's mirror-image script below the drawing) and indeed does approximately state European proportions today. But through the world body proportions vary. Some races, such as the Australian Aborigine, and many African Negro groups, have

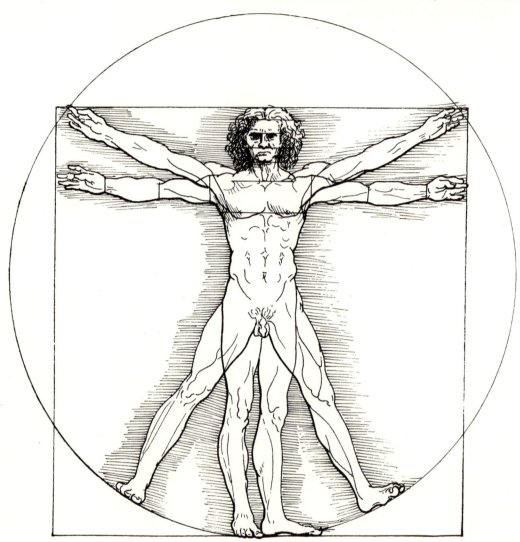

particularly long legs, contributing up to 54 percent of stature, while the axial length (trunk and head) may therefore contribute only 46 percent to stature. At the other extreme are Asiatics, whose leg length may contribute only 45 percent of total stature, and whose axial length some 55 percent (*Fig. 3.2*). That is, Asiatics tend to have short legs and long bodies. Into this group also come the Polynesians — in whom these proportions may still

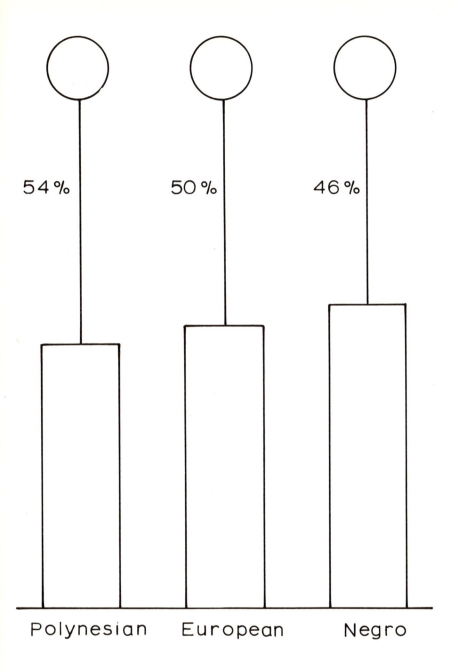

54% 50% 46%

Polynesian   European   Negro

Fig. 3.2: *Characteristic body proportions in Polynesians, Europeans and Negroes. The contribution of axial height (head + trunk) is indicated as a percentage of total height.*

be readily observed, though the tendency towards heavily-muscled lower limbs exaggerates the impression. (Some interesting questions are immediately raised by these Asiatic similarities, but they must take their turn.)

So to generalize, if two individuals, one of European origin and one with Polynesian blood, are seated in identical chairs and then appear to be of the same height, the European will be the taller when they stand. Conversely, if the standing individuals are of the same height, he with Polynesian blood will sit the taller.

The point about these differing body proportions amongst the races of man is that stature equations from long bone lengths must be developed separately for each major race. If a stature equation developed for a lower limb bone of a Negro or a European is applied to Polynesian material then the stature estimate obtained is much below the true stature, because the equation assumes that the measured bone contributes more to total height than it really does. This point is best made by using some additional data obtained by Peter Buck from his physical examination of the Maori Battalion. Buck measured 'segmental limb lengths' on the men and a number of these measurements can be related to measurements of isolated bones of the skeleton. Specifically his data allows us to deduce the length of the femur (thigh bone), tibia (the main bone of the leg) and the radius (one of the two bones of the forearm). When stature equations developed for other races are then applied to these isolated measurements they give an average height for the pure-blooded Maoris of the Battalion from four inches to one and a half inches below the true average height of five feet seven inches, according to which equation is used.

Obviously then, when we come to try and assess the stature of individual New Zealanders from prehistory, none of the standard stature equations developed for other races are adequate, and all will depict New Zealanders as punier than they were. Somehow fresh equations have to be devised. While it would be difficult to exaggerate the difficulties and pitfalls in the way of devising such equations for a prehistoric race whose descendants have inter-married greatly with Europeans, Peter Buck's data on a group we may reasonably regard as being a fairly pure-blooded sample — and certainly the best there will ever be — offers the opportunity to at least develop some equations for Polynesian stature to apply to prehistoric material, and to see how the results accord with early European observation.

The exercise actually proceeded as follows — the steps are much simplified here, and all required the use of a computer.

Firstly, from Buck's data, stature equations were developed

relating length of femur, tibia and radius, to height. Next, these equations were applied to the individual bone lengths of nearly one hundred intact skeletons from New Zealand's prehistoric era. The height of these long-dead individuals was thus calculated. Now, their height being known, it was possible to reverse the process and develop equations relating the lengths of the other main long bones (humerus, ulna, fibula) to height.

Baldly stated like this, the amount of work involved is well concealed. But in the end it was encouraging to find that the average height of these prehistoric men was five feet eight and a quarter inches, in harmony both with early historic observation, and with Buck's impression that his sample from the Maori Battalion was, if anything, rather below the average for the race.

So far we have only dealt with male height, as there seems to exist no specific data on female height in the Maori. But it is consistent throughout the races of mankind that females average 6-7 percent less in stature than males. Remarkable though it may seem, it is statistically valid, with further use of the computer, to create stature equations for prehistoric females as well, from Buck's original data. Using such equations, the average height of a large group of prehistoric New Zealand women was estimated to be five feet three and three-quarter inches — again, compatible with the early records. European female equations would have given this group an average height of five foot three inches, and if Negro only five foot and one inch.

Returning to the point that the average male stature in Europe two centuries ago — and for several centuries preceding that — was five foot two inches to five foot four inches, it is clear that to the European these first New Zealanders were indeed tall people. And the same characteristic existed throughout Polynesia — using these Polynesian stature equations we obtain an average height for a large group of fifteenth century Hawaiian men of five feet eight inches, while women averaged five feet three and a half inches. But the honours, then probably as now, go to the Tongans — the average height of a group of fifteenth century Tongan men is just under five feet ten inches.

We shall return to stature when considering health in prehistoric times, and also origins and relations. Within New Zealand there is not yet sufficient data to reliably comment on differences in stature in different parts of the country, and at different times. At present we don't know of any differences. The people from the famous site at Wairau Bar, on the southern shores of Cook Strait, who lived between the twelfth and fourteenth centuries, averaged about five feet nine inches for the men and five feet four inches for the women. Some fifteenth century Chatham Islanders give about the same figures. Looking at regions, without any time consideration, we find male averages of five feet eight inches for the southern part of the South Island, five feet nine inches for the Canterbury area, five feet nine inches for the East Coast North Island and five feet eight inches for Northland. The impression is of a very similar stature throughout the country.

There are other body proportions to consider in addition to stature and its components, though the information on these is much the best — it is astonishing how little is known about the normal growth and development of the body, as judged by the simplest of measurements. But from modern populations there are some figures to show that Africans as a broad group have proportionately longer arms than Europeans, and Asiatics very slightly shorter arms than Europeans. The greater length of the African arm appears to lie particularly in the forearm. From the past we cannot judge the entire length of arm or leg, but by measuring the individual long bones of the limb it is possible to get a good idea of any differences in proportions between groups. These proportions are best expressed as ratios. In Table 3.1 are given various long bones ratios, such as upper to lower limb, tibia to femur, and so on, for various groups. The figure is a percentage. Thus, an arm to leg ratio of 70 indicates that the arm is 70 percent of the length of the leg.

The suggestion from these figures is that the Polynesians are short in the leg, particularly in the tibia (lower leg), and a little longer than Europeans in the arm, particularly in the forearm. For actual measurements on the living to back this up we again have Surgeon Thomson. Thomson's study continued:

No person can look at a group of New Zealanders and Europeans without at once observing a difference in their figures. This may be produced by some slight alteration or peculiarity in the shape of a bone, or the development of a muscle; but to ascertain clearly what is the cause of this difference in figure between the two races, I carefully measured twenty-three men of each race of similar stature, besides several other men . . . From this examination it appears that the arms of New Zealanders are a little longer than those of a European, and that this difference is caused by an increased length in the forearm and hand. That the legs of New Zealanders are an inch and a half shorter than those of Europeans, and that the greater part of this shortening is found to be in the bones below the knee joint. That the inch and a half which a New

Zealander loses in stature from the shortness of his legs, is made up in his having a longer body.

So Thomson's measurements (Table 3.2) support the evidence of the skeleton. He vividly presents the difference between the groups by describing a Maori in a suit borrowed from a European of the same height; trouser cuffs rolled up, and forearms protruding from the sleeves.

To give a fuller picture of body proportions we should consider also breadth of hip and shoulder. In modern populations we know that Africans tend to be narrow-hipped relative to shoulders, compared with Europeans and Asians. From the past, hip width is readily measured on the intact pelvis, but shoulder width presents a problem, being made up of several smaller bones with much soft tissue. However, some comparison between groups is possible by measuring the length of the clavicle (collar bone) and doubling it. From our rather meagre information it seems that Polynesians are similar to Europeans and Asians in these proportions of breadth — rather broad-shouldered and wide-hipped.

From body proportions to individual bones. As with so many things there is a Eurocentric bias in the books, European anatomy being presented as the anatomy of *Homo sapiens*. It isn't. In details there are considerable variations amongst the various races of mankind. In general the long bones of the arm and leg of the Polynesian are more bowed, more curved, than those of the European (*Fig. 3.3*), and this differing shape has nothing to do with any illness, or dietary deficiency such as that which leads to rickets. It is a distinctive and inherited characteristic of these people. The reasons for bowing of long bones have not yet been satisfactorily elucidated, though there is some evidence that slight bowing offers some mechanical advantage for certain muscles. Bowing is not a result of pulling of powerful muscles, but may be related more to the accommodation of a large and genetically determined muscle bulk. There is no doubt that Polynesians are naturally very muscular. Early Europeans commented on their massive legs: thus Surgeon Thomson:

The limbs of a New Zealander are stout and well-shaped and the calves of the legs are well down, although, from the shortening in the tibiae and fibulae, they look higher up than those of Europeans.

This muscularity seems to be an inherited thing, and not necessarily related to hard physical exercise — the Australian Aborigine could not be said to have led a sedentary life, yet possessed thin shanks and a generally lean body (and a skeletal form very different from both Polynesian and European).

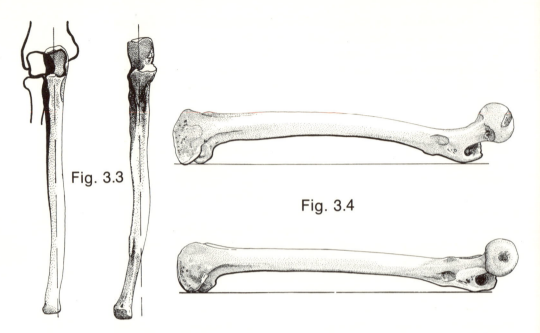

Fig. 3.3

Fig. 3.4

Fig. 3.3: *The Polynesian ulna on the right is more robust and more bowed than the European ulna on the left.*

Fig. 3.4: *The Polynesian femur (above) is more bowed in the shaft than the European femur below.*

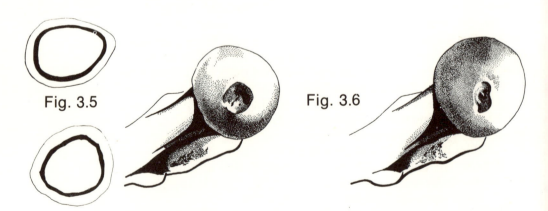

Fig. 3.5

Fig. 3.6

Fig. 3.5: *The upper part of the Polynesian femur (thigh bone) is oval in cross-section, compared with the European femur on the left.*

Fig. 3.6: *The oval fovea on the head of the Polynesian femur contrasts with the usual round fovea of most of mankind.*

In the Polynesian, those that particularly show this bowing are the forearm bones and the fibula of the lower leg, all rather slender bones enveloped in substantial muscles. The femur of the Polynesian also shows marked bowing, again probably to accommodate the massive muscles on the back of the thigh. The femurs of all races show some degree of bowing to accommodate these muscles, but the difference between a Polynesian and a European femur can readily be seen in *Fig. 3.4*. And the Polynesian femur shows other exceptional features. For instance the upper part of the shaft of the bone shows a marked flattening from front to back, so that a cross section of the bone in this upper part is distinctly oval as compared with the round cross-section of other races (*Fig. 3.5*). Again, in the head of the femur, where it fits into the socket of the hip, is the marking of the attachment of a ligament. In most of mankind this marking is circular, and about half an inch across. In the Polynesian it is smaller and distinctly oval (*Fig. 3.6*).

The neck of the femur is the short segment connecting the head, which enters into the hip joint, with the main shaft of the bone. In most of mankind the neck protrudes forward from the shaft at an angle of 10-12°. This is called the angle of torsion, or anteversion. In Polynesians this angle is greatly increased, averaging some 25°, and reaching 45° in some individuals (*Fig. 3.7*).

There must be some functional relationship, not yet worked out, between these various unique, or at least extreme features of the Polynesian femur: that is, there must be something in the action and interplay of the muscles in the hip and thigh that is different in the Polynesian, and requires this different skeletal basis. The problem awaits elucidation, but it is clear that we cannot regard all mankind as having identical anatomy and some of these distinctive Polynesian features must be relevant in the management of some fractures and forms of arthritis in those with Polynesian blood.

The other substantial bone of lower limb, the tibia, has not been looked at as thoroughly as the femur, yet there are obvious differences between the Polynesian form, and others. The shaft of the bone shows the usual tendency to bowing, though it is never as marked as in the femur. The most conspicuous difference is at the upper end where a flat surface — the tibial plateau — enters into the knee joint. In the Polynesian this plateau shows a marked backwards tilting, when compared with the horizontal plateau of other peoples (*Fig. 3.8*). It is possible that this feature is acquired as a result of the continual assumption of the squatting position in a society generally lacking chairs, stools and so on. A lack of

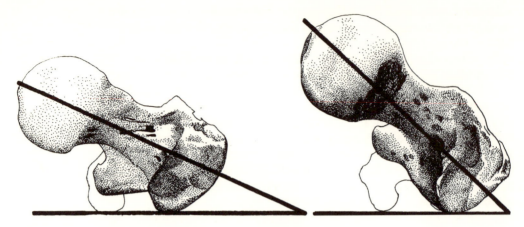

Fig. 3.7: *A Polynesian and a European femur are viewed from their top ends when placed on a flat surface. The neck of the Polynesian femur makes a greater angle with the horizontal – that is, points more forward in the body.*

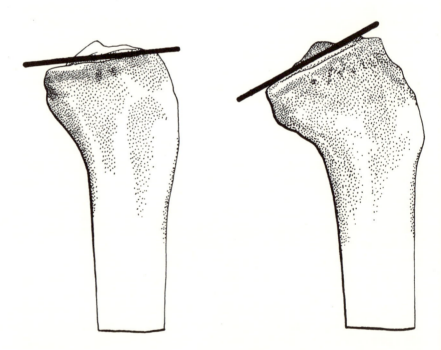

Fig. 3.8: *The tilt of the tibial plateau, where it enters the knee, is much inclined to the horizontal, compared with a European tibia on the left.*

adequate comparative studies makes it impossible to be certain, though the Australian Aboriginal, lacking chairs and so on, has a horizontal plateau.

This is as far as we can go in the story of these differences of body, because most of the work is yet to be done. We can only suggest where other differences may lie, and one of these regions is likely to be the spine, which we know to be longer in the Polynesian, and which may therefore show some structural differences — possibly relevant to modern health. For neither are we yet sure how these features have been handed on to the modern Maori with his admixture of Pakeha blood. There will probably in inheritance prove to be great variation, but the tall stature, the body proportions and the muscularity seem to have survived.

Table 3.1

Various long bone ratios for several groups. Each figure indicates the length of the upper bone of the appropriate pair as a percentage of the lower bone length. Thus, the New Zealand tibia is 80·4 percent of the length of the femur, and is clearly proportionately shorter than in any other group.

		Ratio			
Bones	N.Z.	American Whites	American Negroes	Eskimos	Australian Aborigines
$\dfrac{\text{radius}}{\text{humerus}}$ $\left(=\dfrac{\text{forearm}}{\text{upper arm}}\right)$	78·0	73·8	77·8	73·7	78·3
$\dfrac{\text{tibia}}{\text{femur}}$ $\left(=\dfrac{\text{lower leg}}{\text{thigh}}\right)$	80·4	83·4	86·2	85·5	88·8
$\dfrac{\text{radius + humerus}}{\text{tibia + femur}}$ $\left(=\dfrac{\text{arm}}{\text{leg}}\right)$	71·4	69·8	70·1	71·4	70·2

Table 3.2

Table of average measurements, in inches, recorded by Thomson on 23 New Zealanders and 23 Europeans

		NEW ZEALANDERS Inches	EUROPEANS Inches
1.	Height	67.50	67.50
2.	Tip of the middle finger of the extended right arm and hand, to the same finger of the extended left arm and hand	69.75	69.25
3.	Shoulder to elbow	14.30	14.40
4.	Elbow to the tip of the extended middle finger	18.50	18.00
5.	Shoulder to the hip joint	22.20	22.00
6.	Hip joint to knee joint	16.00	16.00
7.	Knee joint to the ground	18.00	19.30
8.	Shoulder to a line drawn horizontally from the top of the head	11.40	10.30

4. Head Form

We usually recognize people by their faces rather than any proportions of the body and probably, after skin colour, it is the face that is particularly considered when we think of the differences between the races of mankind. Perhaps one of the reasons why the first Europeans felt an affinity with the Polynesians was their facial appearance — vertical in profile, without the protrusion of the teeth often seen in Negroes and some Melanesians, the chin well forward, a flatter nose but a European cast to the eyes: a large head and straight black hair, without the wooliness of other dark skinned races who these early, often fumbling explorers had encountered, sometimes disastrously, around the globe. Even their skins were sometimes no darker than a Nordic with a good sun-tan or a Celt without — Europeans washed with burned umber. This, an attractive culture, skilled traders — trading usually being a mode of diplomacy that Europeans could understand — and the influence of such early Polynesian visitors to Europe as Omai, all add up to the archetypal noble savage of the eighteenth century. The feeling lingers in persistent attempts, to the present day, to bring the Polynesians ultimately out of the Mediterranean, like one of the lost tribes, as if the Pacific or its rim were an unworthy womb for this impressive race.

So we have to look at heads, and heads are complicated.

The measuring of skulls has been a good scientific exercise since Victorian times, and some older scientific journals are packed with impressive, bewildering pages of figures, measurement after measurement, arduously and meticulously obtained by this or that scientific worker. Unfortunately, a great deal of this early work was somewhat sterile in results, for these early workers faced two major problems. The first was the selection of dimensions to measure. Various prominent landmarks on the skull and the measurements between them, came to be accepted as appropriate, but often there was little sound biological basis for the choice. This was not the fault of these serious men, for only in the past decade or so, from experimental work, has a reasonable understanding of the biological basis of skull form started to emerge. Two measurements in particular came to assume immense importance in this major branch of physical anthropology: the length and the breadth of the cranium, and the relationship between them, the cranial index. Thus:

$$\text{Cranial index} \quad = \quad \frac{\text{cranial breadth}}{\text{cranial length}}$$

The range of this index for mankind is from about 70 (= long head) to about 90 (= round head). Various groups of mankind were held to be well defined by their average index, and elaborate patterns of mating and migration were elucidated on the basis of this belief. We shall come later to some earlier comments on Pacific origins and migrations based on the cranial index, but here it suffices to say that there is strong scientific evidence indicating that the dimensions of the vault, and the resulting index are secondary and relatively unimportant things.

The second great difficulty these early workers faced, after the lack of a biological basis for their measurements, was one of interpretation of their masses of figures. Statistical methods and equipment were not adequate to deal with the data, and they struggled against great odds in their attempts to extract sense from them.

In recent years there has been a resurgence of interest in craniology, in the study and measurement of skull form. Part of this resurgence is due to the development of the computer which, together with the development of suitable statistical methods, has allowed a more adequate analysis of cranial data. The influence of the computer has not been entirely good — to some extent it has encouraged an approach of measuring, measuring, in the comforting assumption that the incredible capacity of the computer will, with modern statistics, make some sense of it all, will throw up some gem of knowledge out of the welter of data. The real stimulation to cranial studies has come from anatomists who have microscopically looked at the areas and mode of growth of the skull, and from workers in that field of dentistry called orthodontics, concerned with the way the teeth fit together, who have looked at the problem by means of serial X-ray studies. Out of their work is coming a dynamic, sensible picture of skull form and growth, and we will draw heavily on this sort of work in talking about the Polynesian skull. For make no mistake, the Polynesian head is remarkable amongst mankind — here, more even than in body proportions, the Polynesian is to be placed at one end of the spectrum of the growth and form of *Homo sapiens*.

We have to begin with some terminology.

The names for the different bony parts of the head are used rather loosely, and this probably doesn't matter much. But strictly speaking the entire bony framework of the head is termed the skull, the lower jaw is the mandible and the remainder, the brain-case and face, is the cranium (*Fig. 4.1*). Thus the skull consists of the mandible plus the cranium, and we shall try and be consistent in this terminology here. The top of the cranium, the part that overlies the brain, is the skull-cap, the vault, or calvarium.

When a Polynesian skull is placed beside that of a European, or any other race, differences can be seen. The Polynesian head, particularly of the male, is more angular, appearing distinctly pentagonal when viewed from above or behind, compared with the rounder contour of the European (*Fig. 4.2*). The region of the temples is particularly flat in the Polynesian, and the bridges of bone known as the zygomatic arches stand well clear of the cranial contour, being visible from above (*Fig. 4.3*). In the heads of most races these arches are usually concealed by the cranial contour in this view.

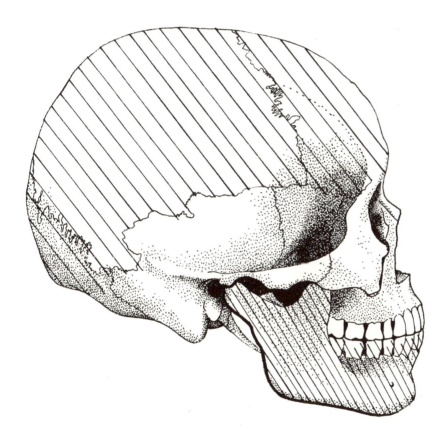

Fig. 4.1: *The basic parts of the head skeleton. The entire skeleton is the skull, the shaded lower jaw is the mandible, and the remainder is the cranium. The shaded upper part of the cranium is the vault.*

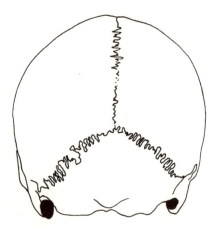
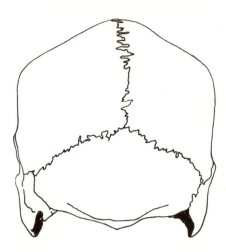

Fig. 4.2: *Compared with the rounded contour of most heads, the Polynesian head is distinctly pentagonal when viewed from behind.*

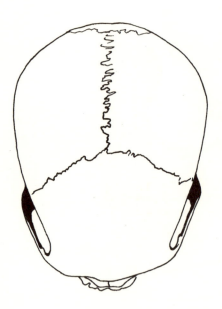
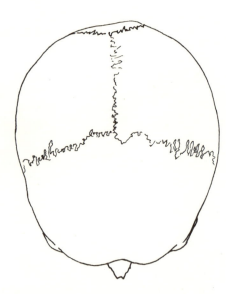

Fig. 4.3: *In the rounder European head the zygomatic arches are not visible from above.*

Viewed from the front the face appears flat-sided, with the cheekbone turning back at right angles to the facial surface. Viewed from the side (*Fig. 4.4*), the face of the Polynesian appears flat, vertical in profile, and not usually with any projection of the front teeth and their supporting bone as commonly seen in Negroes, in whom also the point of the chin may be set back so that the whole of the mid-face region appears to project forward. The vault of the Polynesian cranium is high. And from this side view is seen what is probably the most distinctive Polynesian feature of all, the shape of the mandible. The lower border of this bone shows a continuous and marked convex curve from front to

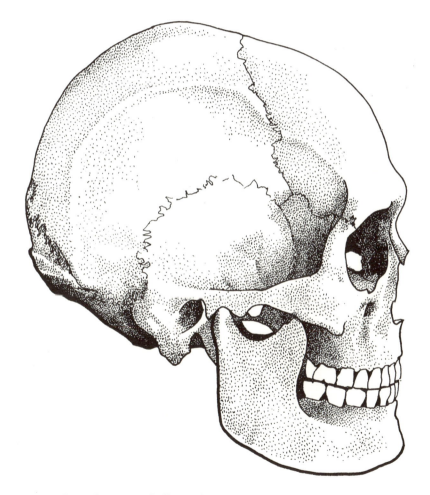

Fig. 4.4: *The Polynesian skull in side view: the vault is high, the profile of the face is vertical, and the jaw is of the 'rocker' form.*

back. This means that when the isolated bone is placed on a flat surface it makes contact by only two points, and therefore rocks when disturbed. This has given rise to the term familiar to Oceanic anthropologists as describing the Polynesian mandible — the rocker jaw.

The unusual form of this Polynesian mandible can be seen when it is compared with the mandibles of other races of mankind, where usually the curve of the lower border of the mandible is interrupted, near its back part, by a distinct notch (*Fig. 4.5*). This is the gonial notch and it allows the delimitation of a process right at the back, the angular process, where some of the powerful chewing muscles are attached. The presence of the notch and the angular process mean that such mandibles are stable when placed on a flat surface — they rest by four points and don't rock. This is the form of mandible found in most of mankind — perhaps 1 or 2 percent of any other race might have a rocker jaw. If you lack Polynesian blood you can clearly feel the notch on your jaw. By contrast the rocker form is dominant in Polynesia (we are talking of prehistory). The figures are a fairly consistent 70 to 80 percent for most groups, and those mandibles which do not rock are usually not far off it — that is, they have insignificant notches and angular processes.

This business of looking at an isolated mandible on a flat surface and observing it to rock is a rather old-fashioned approach — we can see that there is something highly unusual about the bone, but

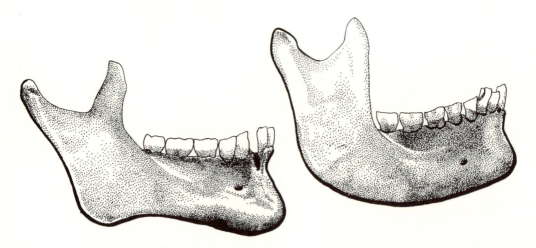

Fig. 4.5: *Most mandibles show a notch in their lower border. By contrast, the Polynesian mandible has a continuous curve to its lower border.*

any explanation for this form cannot arise from contemplation of the bone in this isolated unnatural situation. Enlightenment doesn't lie this way. The bone must be considered as part of the whole skull, and the other parts have to be looked at. Such an unusual jaw *must* indicate some equally unusual cranial form.

But the isolated bone rocking on the flat surface has drawn attention to the unusual shape, and if looked at closely, with a knowledge of what mandibles of other races look like, certain other differences can be seen in the Polynesian mandible. These are illustrated in *Fig. 4.6*. The condyle, which is the part that joins the mandible to the cranium, at the joint under the skull, is inclined forward, whereas the condyles of most mandibles are inclined straight upwards, or backwards. In front of the condyle is the coronoid process to which the temporalis muscle on each side is attached (*Fig. 4.7*). (This is the muscle you can feel moving on the side of your head when you chew.) The coronoid process is particularly large in the Polynesian jaw. And at the front the Polynesian mandible usually shows a distinct arching of the lower border, unlike most other mandibles, which have no distinct arch.

There are other notable features. Polynesian mandibles are massive — only Eskimo mandibles appear to surpass them in size, and then only in some dimensions. In part such massiveness may be related to the demands on the jaw — the tougher the chewing

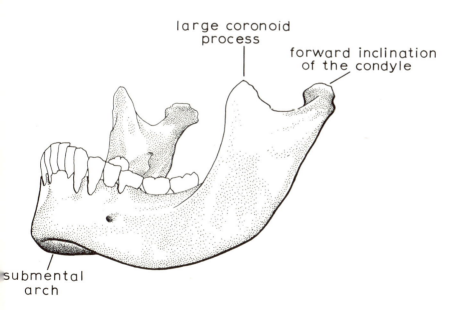

Fig. 4.6: *Features of the rocker jaw.*

Fig. 4.7: *The temporalis muscle on the side of the head attachs to the coronoid process of the mandible.*

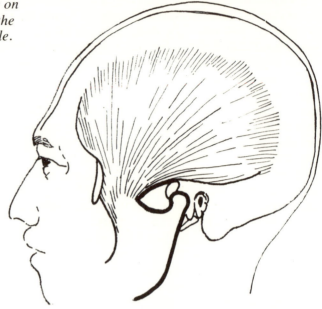

the bigger the jaw. We shall return to this point later, but we can note here that Eskimo mandibles are not usually of the rocker form. This is evidence that the unusual Polynesian form of jaw has nothing to do with the actual physical demands of chewing — how tough the food is, or whatever other demands are made on the teeth.

Considerable time has been spent here in describing the rocker jaw, but with good reason, for this remarkable mandibular form provides the key to understanding how and why Polynesian heads are different. Just before delving further into these differences, two basic observations can be made. The first is that the rocker jaw does not occur in young children, but only starts to appear in late childhood — from about age ten or eleven. Before that age Polynesian children, like any others, show the notched mandible and not the rocker form (*Fig. 4.8*). The second point is that there are two major parts to the mandible, the body and the ramus (*Fig. 4.9*). The angle between these two parts is called the mandibular angle. It is found that in rocker jaws the mandibular angle is consistently smaller than in the non-rocker form — that is, the ramus and body of the Polynesian mandible are set at more of a right angle than the other mandibles, in which the angle is more open (*Fig 4.10*). These two simple findings are clues in the search for an explanation for the rocker form of jaw.

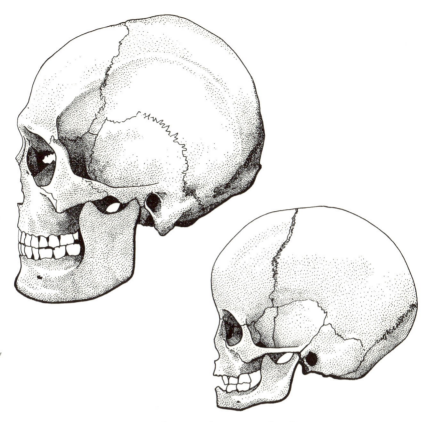

Fig. 4.8: *In early childhood the Polynesian does not have a rocker jaw.*

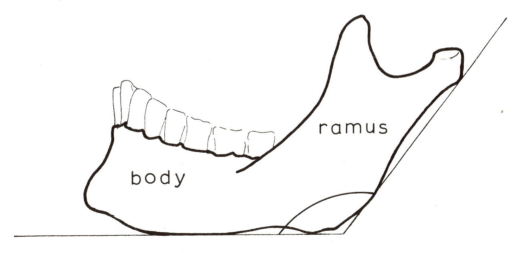

Fig. 4.9: *The two main parts of the mandible and the angle between them (the mandibular angle).*

47

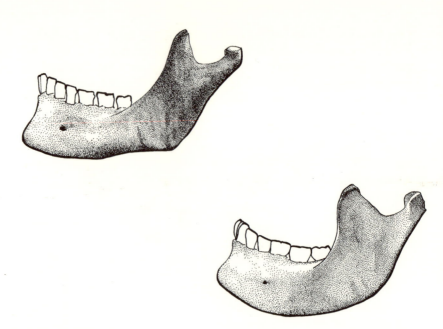

Fig. 4.10: *In the rocker jaw the ramus is more vertical, and forms almost a right-angle with the body of the mandible.*

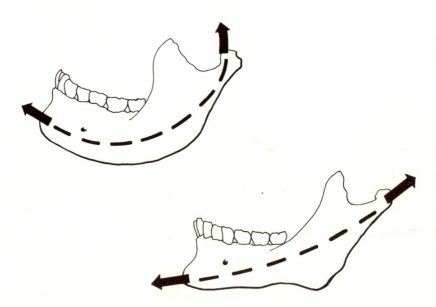

Fig. 4.11: *Showing the more circular direction of growth of the rocker jaw, compared with the straighter growth of most jaws.*

The Swedish dentist Björk studied the growth of the mandible in a large number of children over several years. He implanted metal markers in certain parts of their jaws at an early age, and by following the position of these markers by means of repeated X-rays over many years he was able to reach certain conclusions about the way the mandible grows in different individuals. It has long been known that the condyle is one of the main growth regions of the mandible, which tends to grow away from the cranium almost as though pushed away by bone continually forming at the condyle. What Björk found was that the direction of growth of the mandible away from the cranium varied considerably between individuals. In most individuals the direction of growth at the condyle — the direction of 'push' against the cranium — tends to be backwards, or straight upwards. (This talk of 'push' of mandible against the cranium is convenient, but not really biologically sound.) The mandible then grows down, away from the cranium, in a fairly straight line. This pattern of growth, Björk found, led to the development of the usual form of jaw, with a notch and an angular process.

Though his studies were not in any way directed towards the anthropological problem of Polynesian mandibles, he did find that in a small number of cases the growth at the condyle was directed forwards — the condyle was 'pushing' upward and forward against the cranium. When this pattern occurred the mandible appeared to grow in much more of a circle (*Fig. 4.11*). While he did not specifically comment on it, his illustrations clearly show that in this situation of forward growth at the condyle the result is the development of a rocker form of jaw. We have already seen how the condyle in the rocker jaw is inclined forwards, in evidence of the direction in which it was growing. And the arch under the front part of the Polynesian mandible is further evidence that the bone is curving up in its growth at the front. This more circular growth of the rocker jaw, when compared with the usual form, explains why the former has a more vertical ramus. The arc of the circle of growth sweeps backwards from the condyle, then round and up at the front: whereas in the non-rocker form the direction of growth is downwards and forwards, giving a greater mandibular angle.

In brief, backward or directly upward growth at the condyle gives rise to the usual form of jaw, while forward growth gives rise to a rocker form.

Thus far we have still only considered the mandible as an isolated bone, and not as it is in reality, a unit working in co-ordination with the upper jaw, and the rest of the head. As

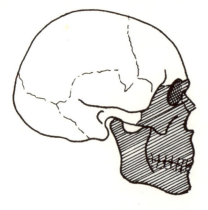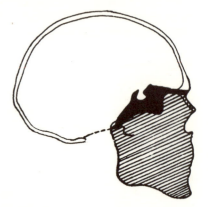

Fig. 4.12: *The head, divided into the facial skeleton (shaded), and the part that encloses the brain. In the section on the right, the cranial base which links the two parts is indicated in black.*

suggested earlier, parts of the body don't develop in isolation, and if there is anything remarkable in any part, then there must be a reflection of it in the other parts with which it interacts. To pursue further the problem of the rocker jaw we now have to look at some simple concepts of cranial anatomy.

The cranium, as we have already defined it, can be divided into the part that encloses and protects the brain (the neurocranium), and the part that forms the skeleton of the face (the viscero-cranium) (*Fig. 4.12*). These two parts are of course joined together, and the area of bone that is common to each, and that separates the brain from the face, is called the cranial base. In man, the neurocranium is above and behind, the viscerocranium is below and in front, and between lies the cranial base.

In quadrupeds, animals that run about on four legs, we find that the spinal cord enters the brain at a slight angle, but the cranial base, on which the brain sits, is essentially flat; the face sits more in front of than below the brain.

In the precursors of man, or in monkeys today, the spinal cord is found to make a greater angle with the cranial base than it does in quadrupeds (*Fig. 4.13*). This is a consequence of course of evolution to an upright posture, be it on the ground or in the trees. The eyes are directed horizontally, and the face starts to drop below the brain. We now find that the cranial base itself is starting to develop a bend, an angle in it. This angle in the cranial base is centred on the little fossa in which the pituitary gland sits, and is called the cranial base angle. The posterior limb of the angle runs from the pituitary fossa to the front of the foramen magnum, through which the spinal cord passes: and the anterior limb runs forward to the bridge of the nose.

When we come to man we find that the face has dropped even further under the brain and neurocranium, and that the cranial base angle is even more pronounced. In most of mankind this angle measures about 130°. However, when we come to measure the cranial base angle in Polynesians we find the average angle to be more than 140°, reaching an extreme of 146° in the extinct Morioris of the Chatham Islands. Table 4.1 shows the cranial base angles measured on several groups of mankind, some modern and some prehistoric. This measurement can only be made by the use of X-rays, which are taken in a standardized way to ensure consistent results.

At this stage we cannot reasonably follow in any detail some rather complicated biological theorizing and experimentation. The gist of it all is that in the presence of this very 'open' cranial

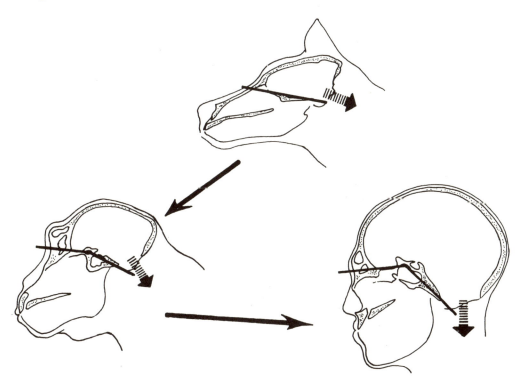

Fig. 4.13: *Evolution of the cranial base angle, from quadruped, through early hominid, to man.*

base angle, an extreme forward growth of the mandible is required if the grinding and cutting surfaces of the teeth are to remain in contact, in occlusion. Now in evolutionary terms it is vital that the teeth occlude, that they fit together properly so that food can be seized and chewed. Only in very recent times has good occlusion ceased to be of paramount importance for survival in the world. We can say, therefore, that the remarkable Polynesian rocker jaw is the reflection of an equally unusual cranial form, the large cranial base angle. The cranial form is to be regarded as primary, for the cranial base develops at a very early stage in embryonic life, and in order that occlusion be maintained the mandible has to grow in the extreme and unusual manner described.

There are still one or two points to clear up. Rocker jaws only appear with the approach of puberty. The reason for this is that the height of the face is also important in determining the direction in which the mandible has to grow to keep the teeth in occlusion. Only in later childhood does the face grow considerably in height, with development of the sinuses in the facial bones that so readily become infected after a cold. Compared with the adult, the infant particularly has a 'collapsed' face with the eyes close to the mouth (*Fig. 4.8*). In the younger Polynesian child the small facial height 'masks' the open cranial base angle. As puberty approaches, the face grows in height, attaining adult proportions, and 'unmasking' the cranial base angle. The large angle is the important factor, but the attainment of adult facial size is necessary for it to be evident in the mandible.

Finally, to go back to the essential difference between rocker and non-rocker jaws: the latter has a notch, with an angular process just behind the notch, and it has been already indicated that some of the powerful chewing muscles are attached to this process. The reason the rocker jaw lacks this process, and therefor the notch, is that the curving form of growth (*Fig. 4.11*) that carries the ramus of the mandible down and back from the condyle, places this part of the bone in the correct position in space for these muscles to be attached without the necessity for a distinct process jutting out.

So much for the rocker jaw. It is a long and intricate story, even here cut short, but this fundamentally different feature of Polynesian people demands adequate explanation for it also contains the explanation for the differing, angular, pentagonal vault. The mandible works as a lever — the third order of lever, for those inclined towards mechanics — and it can be simply demonstrated by a diagram (*Fig. 4.14*) that a mandible with a more vertical ramus, as in the rocker jaw, has a reduced efficiency

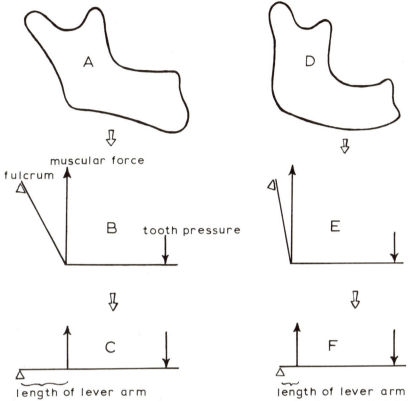

Fig. 4.14: *The mandible as a lever. Non-rocker and rocker jaws (A & D) are represented by line diagrams (B & E), which are in turn mechanically equivalent to levers C & F respectively. The effective length of the lever arm between fulcrum and muscular force is less in the rocker jaw than in the nonrocker form. Therefore in the presence of the rocker jaw a more powerful temporalis muscle is required to achieve the same forces between the teeth.*

compared with a mandible with a more open mandibular angle. In the rocker jaw a larger muscle is therefore required to achieve a comparable force between the teeth, and consequently in the presence of a rocker jaw we find a well-developed temporalis muscle. It appears that in the Polynesian these substantial temporal muscles lead to a flattening of the sides of the skull, which is why the sides appear flat from behind and the cranium appears narrow between the temples in the view from above. The cranium has to expand in advance of the growing brain, and does this particularly by growing upwards, giving rise to a high, flat-sided head.

There is clinical evidence that this concept of the vault shape being determined by the temporal muscles, is correct. Sometimes the temporal muscle on one side has become wasted as a result of some disease process. When this occurs, the skull of the individual shows a markedly reduced coronoid process, and a distinctly rounder contour to the cranium of the affected side. But a word of caution must be added. While it is undeniable that muscles do have an influence on bone shape, it is known that this influence cannot be explained simply as a result of a compressive effect. The influence is there, the mechanism is still unclear. It would be inaccurate to think of the skull as being simply sandwiched and squeezed between two powerful temporal muscles.

To recapitulate (*Fig. 4.15*): in the Polynesian head, an inherited and fixed large cranial base angle sets the upper face down and forward. For the all-important (in evolutionary, survival terms) maintenance of occlusion, the jaw has to grow in a forward direction ensuring a vertical profile to the face. This forward growth also gives rise to the rocker jaw form, whose reduced mechanical efficiency from the point of view of the temporal muscles leads to their marked development. This in turn influences cranial vault shape.

The picture throughout Polynesia is remarkably similar and suggests an origin from a small group of people, a matter discussed in more detail in the next chapter. While this distinctive form has been contrasted with those of other peoples, it cannot be stressed too strongly that all races of mankind present a range of head forms, and what is here described as the usual Polynesian form could be found amongst a large enough number of Scandinavians, Indians or Australian Aborigines, just as prehistoric Polynesians do exist who lack rocker jaws and large cranial base angles. But most Polynesians do show these features and most members of other races do not. It is not a Polynesian 'type' but a form representing one end of the range of skull growth for man, which form most Polynesians happen to have.

It should be noted also that this distinctive head shape is not a consequence of a social custom found in many parts of the world, including some parts of Polynesia — the custom of headbinding. The young head is malleable and adapts to continued pressure, as does the brain beneath, and this curious custom, which must have been regarded as a desirable improvement on nature, has been noted from Melanesia, South and North America, Africa, Egypt, the Orient and Europe. Within Polynesia, headbinding was practised in Hawaii and Samoa until fairly recent times. The

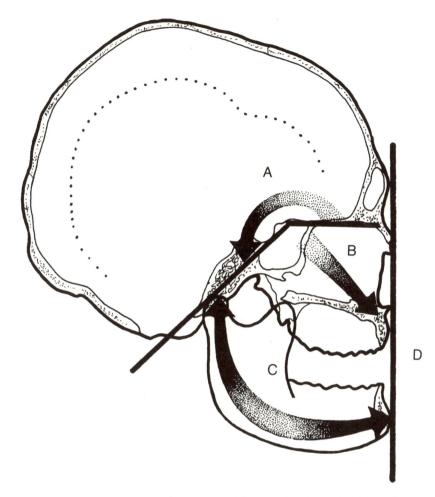

Fig. 4.15: *A summary of the biological basis of Polynesian head form. An inherited, large cranial base angle (A) sets the upper face down and forward (B). In order that occlusion of the teeth be maintained the mandible has to grow in a forward direction (C), leading to the development of the rocker form and ensuring a vertical profile to the face (D).*

technique, in Hawaii at least, involved the binding of padded portions of coconut shell in front and behind the skull during the first two years of life. Depending on the sites where pressure was exerted the head became distinctly compressed and flattened when viewed in profile, or markedly elongated (*Figs. 4.16* and *17*). But the distinctive Polynesian head shape we have discussed is natural and owes nothing to artifice, and there is no evidence that head-shaping was ever practised in New Zealand.

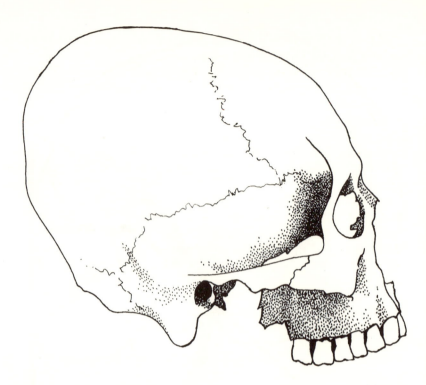

Fig. 4.16: *A flattened head resulting from deliberate moulding in childhood.*

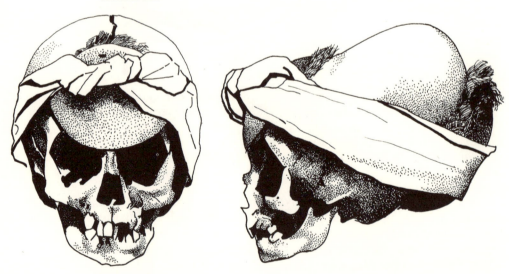

Fig. 4.17: *A method of head-shaping practised in Hawaii. The young head was firmly bound between two segments of coconut shell (after Snow, 1974).*

Within the head there remain the teeth to be considered. As the hardest natural structures in the body they survive well in the ground, and may be fully preserved when bone has largely disintegrated. In prehistoric studies they are invaluable, and there is a great deal to be learned, in anthropological terms, from living populations as well. Teeth can provide information on origins and relationships, age, sex, diet and state of health, and it is possible from a single tooth to build up a picture of an individual — as has been done in the study of human evolution and the precursors of man.

Both the shape and the size of a tooth have a strong genetic background, which is to say that they are inherited, and an analysis of shape and size should allow one to trace relationships between groups. That said, it must be admitted that teeth have not yet played their full part in establishing the pattern of relationships in Oceania. There are several reasons for this. A major one is that the data is inadequate — not nearly enough groups have been studied. In New Zealand, the harsh wear of the diet of the later prehistoric period ensures that tooth shape is usually worn away, and that accurate measurement is impossible. In addition, judgement of many features is subjective and different observers have different criteria. There is a fair bit of confusion in the field.

However, a few comments are worthwhile. On tooth shape, while those who concentrate on such detail recognize a considerable number of traits throughout the dentition, some of great subtlety, most studies mention particularly incisor shape and the cusp pattern on the molars. About 70 percent of Polynesian incisors show in some degree the form picturesquely called 'shovelling' or 'shovel-shaped incisors', in which the back of the tooth, particularly on the upper incisors, is hollowed out (*Fig. 4.18*). Nearly all Chinese show this form, and it is found to an

Fig. 4.18: *Shovel-shaped incisors (drawn from a cast).*

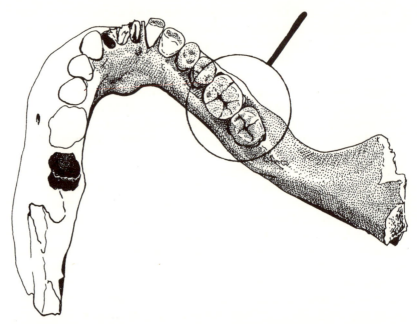

Fig. 4.19: *A mandible showing some features of the molars frequently found in Polynesians. On the right side the first molar has six cusps, and the third molar is absent. The second molar shows four cusps and a + pattern of grooves.*

appreciable extent in some groups of Amerindians, who bear a distant relationship to Asia. Shovelling may be classified as slight, moderate or marked, and a marked degree of shovelling is uncommon in New Zealanders. On the occlusal surfaces of the molars — that is, the surface of each that meets its opposing tooth and between which the food is chewed — grooves delimit complicated patterns of cusps, again with a strong inherited element. Not only are the number of cusps significant but also the manner in which the grooves meet between them. Thus a lower molar can be described as having four, five, or six cusps, while the grooves may form a +, or Y, or X pattern (*Fig. 4.19*). (The grooves are less significant in the upper molars.) New Zealand Polynesian lower molars show a tendency towards a Y groove pattern with five cusps in the first molar, and an + groove pattern with four cusps in the second, but there is a significant incidence (about 15 percent) of first molars with six cusps and this incidence may be traced throughout Polynesia.

In many races it is common to find an additional cusp formed on the side of the upper molars. Called Carabelli's cusp, this is found in some 30 percent of Tongan and Hawaiian teeth, but is practically unknown in New Zealanders. Another variable trait is a tendency towards reduction in size, or absence, of a particular tooth. In New Zealanders the third molar, the wisdom tooth, is absent in some 20 percent of individuals and much reduced in size in a further 20 percent. Even when it is fully formed it often does not occlude with its opposite number to produce an effective chewing surface.

Tooth size is predominately an inherited trait, some races such as the Australian Aborigines having particularly large teeth. There is considerable evidence that, in general, most Melanesians who speak non-Austronesian languages (these are languages not related to Polynesian languages — see Chapter 5) also have rather large teeth, whereas Polynesians, Europeans and Asians have smaller teeth (*Fig. 4.20*). Some elaborate patterns of migration out of Asia into the Pacific have been traced on the basis of tooth size alone, but it is too early to do more than note the ideas. Much more evidence from all the fields of anthropological inquiry is required before such ideas can be taken seriously, or dismissed.

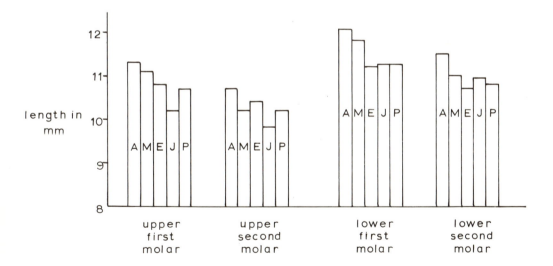

Fig. 4.20: *A graph of the lengths of four molar teeth in five populations. A = Australian Aborigines, M = Melanesian (non-Austronesian speaking), E = European (American White), J = Japanese, P = Polynesian (New Zealand). The Australian teeth are consistently the largest, with the Melanesian usually next in size. The other three groups are consistently smaller.*

Table 4.1

The cranial base angle in several groups.
The Easter Islander and the New Zealanders are Polynesian.

		Cranial base angle	
		number	Mean
1.	Easter Islander	1	149
2.	Norwegian Lapps	61	139
3.	Bantu	101	136
4.	Senegal Negroes	48	135
5.	Bushman	30	134
6.	Japanese	47	133
7.	Swedes	234	132
8.	Danes	102	130
9.	Australian Aboriginals	31	130
10.	New Zealanders	60	142

5. Relations and Origins

We have seen that the first New Zealanders possessed a number of distinct physical features that distinguish them amongst mankind. These features provide some of the clues when we come to look beyond this isolated land for those to whom these people might be related — when we come to look at the story of relationships, migrations and origins.

The early Europeans in the Pacific soon noted that the islands of the eastern half of this vast ocean were inhabited by a fairly homogeneous people. Languages seemed much the same — Cook, on his first and unfortunate day ashore in New Zealand, commented: "Tupia spoke to them in his own language, and it was an agreeable surprise to us to find that they perfectly understood him." Tupaia (the usual modern spelling) was the Society Islander who had embarked on the *Endeavour* in those islands. Much later Cook commented: "I collected a great many of their words, both now and in the course of our former voyage; and being equally attentive, in my inquiries, about the language of the other islands throughout the South Sea, I have the amplest proof of their wonderful agreement, or rather identity."

The physical similarities were also clear and in contrast to the Melanesians (as they are now known) to the west. Forster, Cook's scientist on the second voyage, described the differences:

> We chiefly observed two great varieties of people in the South Seas, the one more fair, well-limbed, athletic, of a fine size, and a kind benevolent temper; the other blacker, the hair just beginning to become woolly and crisp, the body slender and low, and their temper, if possible, more brisk, though somewhat mistrustful. The first race inhabits O Taheitee, and the Society Islands, the Marquesas, the Friendly Isles, Easter Island and New Zealand. The second race peoples New Caledonia, Tanna and the New Hebrides, especially Mallicollo.

Others came to comment on similarities in customs and material things, and eventually someone drew in the Polynesian triangle, Hawaii, Easter Island and New Zealand at the corners and with the western boundary passing between Tonga and Fiji, and between the Ellice Islands and the Gilberts (*frontispiece*). Within this triangle the similarities of men are impressive, and we shall look first at the evidence for relationships and migrations within this region.

Such evidence comes from a sophisticated analysis of various similarities; the evidence of language, of customs and beliefs, of oral traditions (for there is no writing in Polynesia apart from the *rongorongo* script of Easter Island, which may be post-European) and of artefacts, material things such as fish hooks, adzes, ornaments, houses, canoes, and so on. All these things must be considered as well as the people themselves. W. W. Howells has commented that a physical anthropologist walks softly amongst linguists, to which must be added that here there may also be a stumbling amongst artefacts; but some general statements must be attempted.

Firstly the evidence of language, for there is no doubt that the study of the languages of Polynesia has been one of the most enlightening sources of information about the relationships and origins of these people. More — it can reasonably be said that from such study has come the basic framework of modern views on these relationships. The framework will be filled out and doubtless modified in many respects by information from the other sources, but it is unlikely that the broad reconstruction of Polynesian movements as indicated by language will be proved grossly wrong. (Beyond Polynesia, to the west, the pattern of language is much less clear, as we shall see.)

Linguists have various approaches to the analysis of languages to determine how closely they are related. The general structure — the grammatical rules, and the sounds used — may be compared. It is fairly obvious, even to the linguistically innocent, that the Polynesian languages have similar words for similar things, with the vowel sounds particularly remaining the same but with the consonants becoming modified or even eliminated. Examples of this are given in Table 5.1, taken from Peter Buck's *The Coming of the Maori,* where the similarities are as clear as many that may be observed between the Romance languages of Europe. Another linguistic approach, termed lexicostatistics, endeavours to determine the number of shared words amongst languages that are believed to have a common origin. Related to this is glottochronology, which assumes that as languages separate, words in them are replaced at a fairly constant rate. For example, about 80 percent of the original basic vocabulary is believed to survive after a thousand years. If two languages separated from a common stem at that time, then after a thousand years they will share about 64 percent of their basic vocabulary; this figure because the same words will not — or not necessarily — be replaced in each language, and the calculation becomes 80 percent of 80 percent = 64 percent.

The problems and complications are considerable, but the

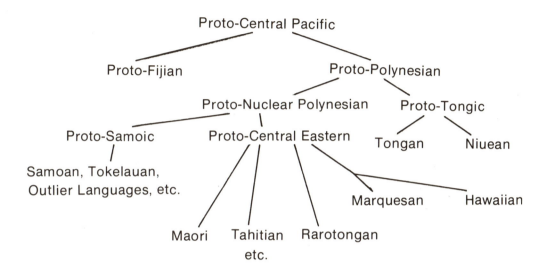

Fig. 5.1: *A classification of Central Pacific Languages (after Pawley and Green).*

conclusions seem clear. Within the Polynesian triangle the languages are closely related, and it is possible not only to derive the order in which the languages separated from a common forebear, but to suggest the times of subsequent diversification. In *Fig. 5.1* such a developmental tree of origins and relationships is given for the major Polynesian languages. At the trunk lies the common forebear, the prototype of the Polynesian languages, therefore termed Proto-Polynesian. This no longer exists as an individual language, but from the many common words in its descendants it can reasonably be reconstructed. Even more, from these surviving common words a description of the island or islands of origin filters through. This description points to a high island group of the West Polynesian-Fiji area, with the period of development and emergence of Proto-Polynesian as a language probably starting about 1000 BC. So it is possible that the cradle is a little further west, in Fiji, just outside the triangle.

The Polynesians, then, came out of the west, and Buck's *Vikings of the Sunrise* is a bit of poetic licence. Proto-Polynesian in turn split into two languages about 500 BC; Proto-Tongic, the forerunner of modern Tongan and Niuean, and proto-Nuclear Polynesian, the forerunner of some twenty-five remaining languages including Maori. Western Polynesia — including Samoa and Tonga — was the scene of these events, but on linguistic evidence no identification of a specific island in the region is possible. Nevertheless, after evolving in the area for perhaps five hundred years, proto-Nuclear Polynesian split into proto-Samoic, the forerunner of modern Samoan, which obviously stayed put, and proto-Outlier and proto-Eastern Polynesian, which constitute, respectively, evidence for the drift to the west into Melanesia, and the push to the east into the Marquesan-Society Island region of Central-East Polynesia. These splits are dated to the first five hundred years of the Christian era by linguists. Finally, in the next five hundred years, AD 500-1000, came the eastern diaspora, to Easter Island, Hawaii and New Zealand — and possibly in that order in time. Proto-Eastern Polynesian is therefore the grandparent of all the eastern Polynesian languages, and it is not surprising that Tupaia was understood in New Zealand. On this evidence, the first New Zealanders should be most closely related to other eastern Polynesians, including those of the Cook Islands, through which the migration(s) may have passed. The relationships with Tonga and Samoa should be more distant, while, furthest away just outside of the western limits of Polynesia, is the Fijian connection.

After linguistics, there is much other evidence, perhaps less readily parcelled and dated than languages, but attesting to the close relationships within the triangle. Of course not every feature is common to all. In the realm of gods and heroes we find, for example, the names (modified according to the language) of Tangaroa, Tu, Tane and Tiki. Tangaroa was God of the sea, Tu was involved in the separating of the earth and the sky, Tane was God of the forest, or of wood carving, while Tiki was the first male. The human mediums of the gods were tohunga, and the religious areas or enclosures were marae, characterized by boundaries, or at least features of stonework. The concepts of tapu and mana are similar throughout. In material things there are similarities in fish hooks and other fishing gear, in food pounders and in adzes. The similarities are sometimes gross, sometimes subtle, and are closer between the island groups of the east, but they are pervading. There is no denying the essential oneness of the Polynesian people.

But in the final analysis, people are the essence and the ultimate evidence should be with them — the form of the living and the remains of the dead. Theoretically, the answers to relationships and origins should lie here and not with languages, customs or creations, for people are the core, and physical characteristics are inherited according to biological rules, unlike the less ruly features of language and material things.

This is the theory, but as always, matters are not so simple. For one thing the pattern and rules of inheritance of many features are still imperfectly understood. Genetical studies on fruit flies, or mice, are legion, but man is considerably more complicated, and breeds slowly and not to order. Living Polynesians may not be ideal sources of biological information about the past — two or three centuries of European involvement in the Pacific have seen to that. The mixing of genes since the earliest days of sailor, whaler and missionary has been extensive and unpredictable in effect. Modern tests allow great refinement of analysis of blood groups and blood proteins, but the more subtle the analysis the greater the chance of it being obscured by genetic mixture. On the broadest scale we know that Polynesians lack blood group B almost entirely, but as we get into finer and finer analysis of such things as blood proteins we cannot be sure that they are telling the truth. A number of years ago the major authority on blood groups in the Pacific concluded, somewhat in despair: "Blood group genetical studies do not tell us the racial components of the Pacific peoples or their paths of migration." So we can only look at the living in very general terms.

The prehistoric skeletal record is uncontaminated by foreign genes, but offers its own problems. Particularly here the mode of inheritance of many features is uncertain. An individual's skeletal appearance, called his phenotype, is formed not only by the combination of genes received from his parents (constituting his genotype), but also the erratic effects of environment. We have to be very cautious in using some physical features as genetic markers for a human group. For example in parts of New Guinea there might seem to be a clear genetic difference between the pygmies of some inland areas and the taller coastal people. But if brought to the coast young, and fed a decent diet, the 'pygmies' grow up tall. So we can assess innumerable skeletal features, subject them to statistical analysis and come up with charts of relationships — but we are not always sure as to the relative significance of inheritance and environment, of the "seed or the soil", on these features. For these reasons the assessment of relationships within Polynesia from skeletal remains is far from being sorted out. At present conclusions are tentative, and there is a final and major reason for this — a dearth of well-excavated, substantial skeletal series, dated and comparable between island groups.

Assessing relationships from bones is really just an extension of the everyday observation that features run in families, that children resemble their parents in face and in body build, or, on a larger scale, that some groups tend to have fair hair and fair skin, others dark hair and swarthy skin and so on. Bones show similar inherited features and these can be assessed, analysed statistically, and a measure of the closeness of relationship of groups — their 'biological distance' — obtained.

Most skeletal studies of the biological distance between groups use data from the skull, because this is the most complicated bony structure, contains the most information, and possibly is least subject to environmental influences — in other words it is more probable that inheritance is coming through unimpaired in many features of the skull than in the rest of the skeleton. Two different forms of data may be used from the skull. The first involves measurements of distances and angles between various landmarks. For example, two measurements we could use would be the cranial base angle, and the angle between body and ramus of mandible. As noted before this is a pastime indulged in since Victorian days, and one which has led to writings of paralysing boredom, pages and pages of figures and statistical computations devoid of biological meaning. But approached with a modern understanding of skull form and growth, which we have already discussed, and using measurements selected on the basis of this understanding, it can be a most fruitful and revealing method of analysis.

The second form of data is obtained from the skull not by measuring but by noting the presence or absence of some minor feature, or the extent of its development. *Fig. 5.2* gives an idea of some of the features that may be thus recorded. The dental features we have looked at earlier are valuable here — molar cusp patterns and shovel-shaped incisors, and several others. The variation of these bony and dental features is seldom, if ever, of significance in evolutionary — that is, selective or survival — terms, and obviously is most akin to observing families with big noses, small ears, and so on. As might be expected from this analogy, this sort of data is more likely to be of value in assessing relationships between apparently closely related groups than between groups far removed from one another. These data are called 'discrete' or 'non-metric', as opposed to 'metric' data which are probably more significant in revealing connections between people who are not closely related.

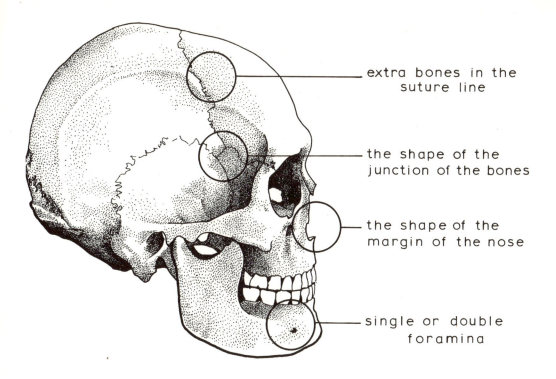

extra bones in the
suture line

the shape of the
junction of the bones

the shape of the
margin of the nose

single or double
foramina

Fig. 5.2: *Examples of the features that may be assessed when estimating relationships between individuals and groups.*

As with languages, the convenient way of setting out the results of such an analysis of skull form, metric or non-metric, is in the form of a tree. The closer together two groups are on the branches the closer their relationship, and all may be traced through to a common stem or trunk. Data from other parts of the body, such as body proportions or selected features of the limb bones, may be used in an analysis, provided there is some understanding of the way in which the features are inherited.

Even a superficial look at the skeletal form of the prehistoric people of the Polynesian triangle suggests a remarkable sameness, an homogeneity of form throughout — allowing that the skeletal record is incomplete and that there is archaeological and linguistic evidence of the penetration of Melanesia into the western fringes of Polynesia. But from island groups as distant in space and in time as Tonga, Samoa, the Marquesas, Hawaii, Easter Island and New Zealand, the physical pattern already described is pervading: tall, robust people with long bodies, short legs, bowing of limb bones, and a number of distinguishing features to these bones, particularly the upper end of the femur: vertical faces in profile, a large cranial vault of distinctive shape, and a remarkable jaw form. The incidence of rocker jaws is about 80 percent throughout Polynesia. Bear in mind that the incidence of this jaw form, with all its implications for cranial form and growth, probably occurs in only 1-2 percent of other groups of mankind.

When some of these features are fed into the great statistical mincing and parcelling machine, the homogeneity, the sameness, is confirmed. In some studies of mandibles from throughout Polynesia the computer has been unable to separate material from the different island groups. Other studies cluster all Polynesian heads tightly together when compared with other groups. But an analysis of a large series of Polynesian skulls by M. Pietrusewsky did separate the various groups in a manner that in some respects fits with the story provided by archaeology and linguistics. To recap, these other sources indicate that the Polynesians, or their forefathers, came from the west, with Tonga and Samoa being among the first islands settled within the triangle. Archaeological excavations suggest that after moving through Fiji by as far back as 1500 BC, they were on Tonga and Samoa and other islands of West Polynesia before about 1000 BC. Then came the great push eastward, with the Marquesas and maybe other parts of Central East Polynesia being reached in the first five hundred years of the present era. From these eastern centres came the diaspora, north to Hawaii, south-east to Easter Island, and south-west to New Zealand, these migrations occurring soon after AD 500.

Pietrusewsky's analysis is set out in *Fig. 5.3*. Some clusters fit satisfactorily when compared with the archaeological and linguistic story. For example, using non-metric data from the skulls, Fiji, Tonga and Samoa were found to be most similar. Again, the Tuamotus and the Society Islands, as might be expected, were associated, and also close together were the Marquesas, Hawaii, Easter Island and New Zealand. However, his analysis of the metric data produced some problems — the New Hebrides, a Melanesian island group, were placed closer to New Zealand and the Marquesas than were Tonga and Samoa.

These discrepancies are unsurprising, and this analysis from head form is unlikely to be improved on for some time — immediately there is little point in trying to improve on it, for the means are not there. That is, much of the material used was culled from museum collections around the world, collected at various times by various itinerants, fossickers, missionaries and so on. By modern standards it has little known position in time — and

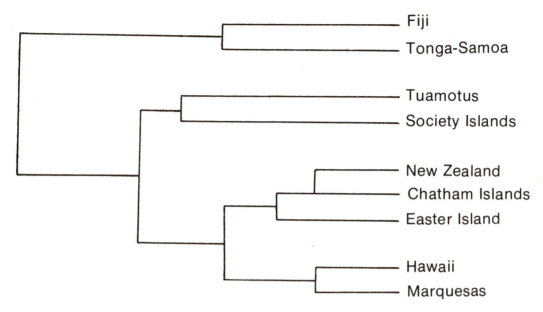

Fiji

Tonga-Samoa

Tuamotus

Society Islands

New Zealand

Chatham Islands

Easter Island

Hawaii

Marquesas

Fig. 5.3: *Relationships of Polynesian groups and Fiji, derived from 'discrete' head features (after Pietrusewsky).*

knowing museum collections, even the place of origin cannot always be assured. Two or three populations, two or three migrations over five hundred or a thousand years of time, could be bundled into one group for this exercise. The marvel is really that the agreement with language and archaeology is so good. Until well-excavated and dated skeletal material from a sufficient number of areas emerges, this analysis must suffice.

All our sources, therefore, tell a broadly similar story of the settlement and relationships within Polynesia. What can be said about where the Polynesians came from, beyond Polynesia — of their 'ultimate origins', to use a not-entirely-desirable phrase? The picture now becomes much hazier, much less certain — about the most certain thing of all is that further studies in linguistics, in archaeology and in physical anthropology, will much clarify it.

It is necessary to persevere just a little longer with the names of languages. Linguists identify the Proto-Polynesian language as having separated from a subdivision of the great Austronesian language family, which embraces just about all the languages of the Pacific, with the exception of those of Australia and most of New Guinea as well as a few islands east of New Guinea.

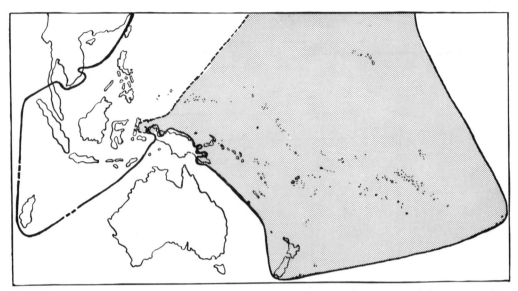

Fig. 5.4: *The limits of the Austronesian language family are indicated by the continuous line, extended to Madagascar in the west. The Eastern Austronesian or Oceanic division lies within the shaded area.*

This is shown in *Fig. 5.4*. This father, or perhaps grandfather, of Proto-Polynesian is called Eastern Oceanic. One plausible homeland for the part (Proto-Central Pacific) to which Fijian and Polynesian belong seems to be in the northern New Hebrides region. From this centre, descendant languages spread, north and west into Micronesia and Melanesia, and east into Fiji and Polynesia.

Archaeology equates the easternmost of the Oceanic speakers, in Fiji and Polynesia, with a form of pottery called Lapita, characterized by certain dentate-stamped designs (*Fig. 5.5*). The pottery, however, has a wider distribution, through much of island Melanesia (*Fig. 5.6*). Moreover, the movement seems to be from west to east (that is, out of Melanesia), and fairly rapidly in the middle part of the first millenium BC. However, only in the east can Lapita ware tentatively be identified with any particular speakers of a proto-language.

In the east, then, these careless housekeepers seem to qualify as the ancestors of the Polynesians — as the pre-Polynesians. By the time they stopped making such pottery — it is known now from both Tonga and Samoa — they were physically Polynesians. In the east, by which we mean the western fringes of Polynesia, there is evidence now (from the Lau islands south-east of Fiji,

Fig. 5.5: *An example of Lapita pottery, from Melanesia.*

facing Tonga) of people fully Polynesian in physical form, associated with Lapita sherds, and dated to about 500 BC.

But *their* origins are obscure. They came into this eastern Oceanic area — from where? Remember that language (and some archaeology) suggests a diffusion from this area out into Micronesia and western Melanesia. The questions are just about all unanswered, and this area is at present the focus of study by scholars of the various disciplines. Some would trace them, pretty much Polynesians already in physical form, a sea-going people, out of Indonesia, skirting the larger islands of Melanesia, and somehow or other preserving the purity of their genes in their eastward progress — a remarkable feat. Others would bring them directly locally out of Melanesia, a possibility firmly denied by the American physical anthropologist W. W. Howells, who from a long acquaintance with the area and the problems, would prefer to bring them out of Asia through Micronesia — a suggestion which archaeologists and linguists feel most uncomfortable about. The questions lie on the table. The answers lie in the ground. Little human skeletal material has been excavated in association with Lapita pottery. Perhaps, as the reports increase, such material will be found further west showing significantly those skeletal features with which we are familiar as representing the Polynesians. But again, perhaps not. In searching for the 'ultimate origins' of the Polynesians it may be necessary to look no further than Fiji, if we agree that a people are to be ultimately defined not by how they speak or what they make, but by their appearance. That is, people define themselves.

The point is that skeletally Polynesians are so similar that we can say with considerable confidence not only what the first Polynesians looked like, but that the founding group must have been small. It could have been extremely small. Some recent computer studies, based on data from Pacific populations, have shown that as few as six people of child-bearing age could have an almost 50 percent chance of surviving the risks of life and establishing a viable population, not headed for extinction. If the founding fathers and mothers are increased in total to only fourteen the chances of survival improve greatly. Now any

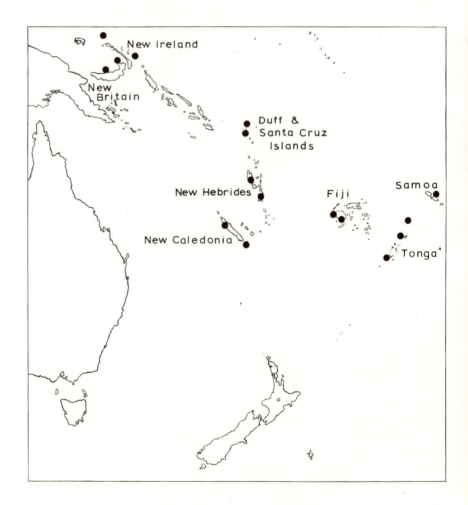

Fig. 5.6: *Location of the principal Lapita sites at present known in island Melanesia and Western Polynesia; the dark circles indicate the sites.*

half-dozen or so people plucked out of a population may poorly represent the average physical form of that population — rocker jaws are found in India and Scandinavia, but are not there the usual form. (No, I am *not* suggesting a Scandinavian or Indian origin for the Polynesians.) But the first Polynesians may have been a canoe-load of closely-related people cast upon the then uninhabited Fiji, not at all typical of the population from which they sprang. (And while Melanesians and Polynesians may now be different, we really know nothing about Melanesian, using the term as a region, physical form of four thousand years back.) Eastern-Oceanic speaking and Lapita-making, they became at that moment the Polynesians. They would not of course have seen themselves in such dramatic light, and it would have been a remarkable (though not unimaginable) canoe that carried the entire armamentarium and paraphenalia of Polynesian life — pigs, dogs, rats, chickens, breadfruit, yam, taros, gourds, bananas and so on. Some of these could have been acquired in later contact with the west, when a larger Polynesian population was more resistant to the impact of new genes.

So the 'ultimate origins' may be little beyond the Polynesian triangle. The Polynesian form could have been plucked by drift of genes and canoes out of the populations inhabiting island Melanesia some four thousand years ago. I incline to this view myself at present. It must be emphasized that continuing work in archaeology and linguistics in this complex part of the Pacific is likely to greatly clarify the picture in the next few years and from skeletal material will come some of the most valuable information. The suggestions of a direct Mongoloid origin of the Polynesians, skirting islands and indulging in linguistic but not physical intercourse, must not be overdone. The heads are not the same, on very limited evidence the legs are not the same, the body proportions are not all the same, and it is most unwise to settle on a few dental features such as shovel-shaped incisors and present them as proof. Anyway, whatever their origins, in the east the now distinctive Polynesians flourished and spread. Those who remained in the west later received a smattering of Melanesian genes — Melanesian, that is, as we now define the term. Perhaps we should not leave this interface between Polynesia and Melanesia with such a facile phrase as a 'smattering of genes'.

Fijians are said to be basically Polynesian in physical characteristics, with some later admixture and blending of Melanesian traits. The Tongans are said to be Polynesians with just a hint of contact with Melanesia. The truth is that there is little skeletal information, or at least study of it, to prove or disprove such statements. But it must be said that there *are* skeletal differences, grossly detectable, without elaborate statistics, between Eastern and Western Polynesia. In plain figures the incidence of rocker jaws, with all the implications for head form, is similar in each part: but the western jaw is a less exaggerated form of the trait, and differences are apparent, particularly on X-ray. Again, the Western femur shows the Polynesian features we have looked at earlier, but, particularly in the flattening of the upper shaft, the features are often less pronounced. This is unsurprising, however, and need not necessarily imply a later 'smattering' of Melanesian genes. The progressive settlement of the islands of Polynesia involved again and again and again the genetic concept of the 'founder effect', wherein any small group may be atypical of their population of origin, and lead to a subsequent new population perceptibly different. This, rather than Melanesian genes, may account for the observable differences between East and West in the Polynesian triangle.

These thoughts — they are little more — on Polynesian origins, may be astray. Fortunately there is no predicting what the next ten years will show, and perhaps a trail leading back to the west will be found. In the meantime there is the theoretical possibility, really quite comforting in its simplicity, that for origins we need scarcely look beyond Polynesia itself.

Note that there seems no place, from the modern evidence, for the concept of an American origin for the Polynesians. For modern romance and superb publicity Heyerdahl deserves top marks, but the scientific evidence points the other way. For example Heyerdahl leant heavily on evidence from Easter Island for his theory of American Indian settlement of Polynesia, yet R. Murrill, after studying the human remains from Heyerdahl's excavations there, concluded that the Easter Island people were Polynesian from the time of first settlement. This is only one of many, many lines of evidence disproving Heyerdahl's thesis. There are more fantastic ideas still afloat, Polynesians out of Mesopotamia, Arcadia, shipwrecked Spaniards or whatever, that rightfully belong in the nineteenth century. Why these stories should still attract attention is conjectural. The Polynesian canoe needs no gilding. The story is romantic enough without introducing fantasy.

Having scanned Polynesia and a bit beyond, we can now focus on New Zealand. Some accounts suggest that the first Polynesians found the land already occupied by another people, the Maruiwi. The origins of these first people are obscure. According to Te Matorohanga, these people were tall and upright, with large bones, prominent knees, flat faces, slant eyes, flat noses, expanded nostrils, straight hair and reddish-black skin. This sort of information was interpreted by early anthropologists such as Percy Smith and Elsdon Best as indicating that the Maruiwi were of Melanesian origin, a view supported by early workers in physical anthropology. Thus Professor J. H. Scott of the Otago Medical School, at the conclusion of a monumental craniological study that is still of some value ninety years later: "If any further proof were needed of the mixed origin of the Maori race, it is given in this paper . . ."

My own reading of the physical description given above is that it is eminently Polynesian: the only incongruous note sounded is some pages later in Percy Smith's account, when he says they had thin calves. As Peter Buck mischievously notes: "The Matorohanga school was able to create physical differences, but its linguistic range was not sufficient to introduce differences in language and so the Melanesian origin is also contradicted by the first settlers not only bearing Polynesian names but applying them to their first canoes and places they occupied."

Furthermore, some of the traditions suggest that the Maruiwi were driven south, to the southern part of the South Island, then out to the Chatham Islands, by the new arrivals. This being so, one would expect the Morioris of the Chathams to show clearly non-Polynesian features and to be markedly different from the later mainland dwellers. The reality is otherwise. All the body features we have described are seen in very marked form in the Moriori and they have the highest incidence of rocker jaws in Polynesia. The Morioris are the most Polynesian of Polynesians. They are far removed from any Melanesian people, at least of modern form.

This is not the place to discuss the value of traditions in interpreting the past, nor would I be remotely competent to do so. Obviously in this context they can no more be taken as absolute and literal guides then can parts of the Bible. They form part of the evidence and must be used judiciously. (The Maruiwi 'traditions' have been shown to be a fabrication.) One problem is that some early European scholars seemed determined to fit the stories from different tribal areas into one coherent whole, and produced a fiction that is still being presented today as the reality, when it is in fact but a Pakeha mish-mash. For example the story served up in many texts is that New Zealand was discovered by Kupe, who came from Hawaiki about AD 900. He found the land uninhabited (though there is some divergence of opinion here) and after living here for a number of years (seventy, by one account) departed again, from Hokianga for Hawaiki. The next visitor was Toi, a chief of Hawaiki, who reached New Zealand with a crew of sixty men, in search of his grandson who had disappeared at sea. Now, when the various tribal versions are examined it is found that some refer back to Kupe, and some to Toi. In no one tribal version do both appear, and to put them together in a potted prehistory is wrong.

The greatest of the traditional events is, of course, the coming of the Great Fleet from Hawaiki, which occurred, as every schoolboy knows, in AD 1350. It is from the canoes of the fleet that the modern impressive genealogies originate. However, David Simmons, in a close analysis of the Great Fleet story, using early written Maori texts, comes to the conclusion that there was no such major migration from Hawaiki, in the sense of some specific place within eastern Polynesia, and that the story may refer to a later dispersal of canoes from Northland to other parts of the country. Some genealogies dating from the 'Great Fleet' go back fourteen generations: others, twenty-three generations. Obviously the same migration is not being referred to. It is worth repeating that what modern studies challenge are not so much the immensely absorbing and important traditional stories, but the early European distortion of them. The traditions have undoubtedly much valuable information to offer in the unravelling of prehistory, but obviously it is only those fluent in the language of the area and capable of going back to the earliest texts recorded in European times who can undertake such interpretation. Such investigators also need a sound grasp of the other evidence from prehistory. These people do not abound. The bowdlerizations of the tribal traditions that frequently appear in popular books do obscure much richness from the past.

After all this, what does the physical evidence tell?

There does seem to be a remarkable similarity of body form throughout the country over a period of nearly a thousand years. The earliest skeletal material comes from Wairau Bar, the famous site on the southern shores of Cook Strait, excavated by Roger Duff of the Canterbury Museum in the 1940s and 50s. The first human material from this site is dated to about AD 1150. From a similar or slightly later period comes a limited amount of material from Opito on the Coromandel peninsula, and Castlepoint on the Wairarapa coast. Inspection of this material has so far revealed (the work done is inadequate) no gross differences from individuals living over the next few hundred years, up to the early part of the last century. They all conform to the pattern, to the overall body form earlier described, and there is no convincing, and

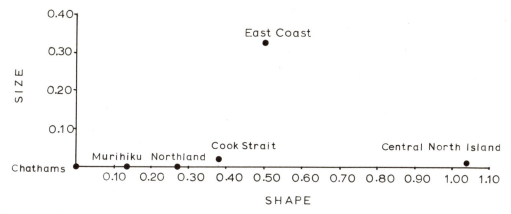

Fig. 5.7: *The biological distances between different regional groups in New Zealand, using measurements from mandibles and Penrose's 'Size and Shape' statistic. The term 'size' here is a statistical concept, not strictly comparable with size as directly observed. The East Coast and Central North Island regions stand out as being rather different from the other groups.*

minimal suggestive evidence, of the introduction of other genes, and the entrance into the country of different people, since the earliest days. Put another way: on the present evidence the first settlers in New Zealand were Polynesian as we now understand the term, and if several episodes of settlement took place then these later settlers were physically very similar and presumably came from much the same group of islands.

When we consider how very similar Eastern Polynesians now are after several hundred years of separation, it would be unsurprising for us to find it difficult to sort out, after several hundred years, the separate groups that may — or may not — have arrived on these shores from several island origins in the east of the triangle.

This impression of similarity in New Zealand can be subjected to a statistical analysis. *Fig. 5.7* shows the picture obtained when measurements from a large series of male mandibles are interpreted by a particular distance statistic, called, after its originator, Penrose's Size and Shape Statistic. It attempts to indicate how closely people of the various groups are related. (The material has all the defects mentioned for the wider, Pacific study of heads — particularly a lack of placement in time.)

The two axes of the graph, size, and shape, need not be regarded as particularly important here. Rather it is the general spread of the groups that concerns us. The Chatham Islanders have been used as the base group, though any other group could have been used instead. The analysis does confirm the general impression that the Chathams and the Murihiki groups are closest in form, with not much separation from other parts of the country except for the East Coast of the North Island and the central North Island, which stand apart. Analysis of a female group of mandibles gave a similar picture, except that the central North Island was not represented.

These are only beginnings, but on this data one can suggest that if any parts of the country stand out as being slightly different in human terms, in prehistory, it is not the Chatham Islands but the East Coast and the central North Island. Here the genes may be different, and settlement time and source may be different. There is some other evidence, particularly linguistic, of the distinctiveness of the East Coast region. But, as Peter Buck comments: ''A more comprehensive survey of the physical characters of the different Maori tribes is needed to shed light on the problem.'' If any progress in these studies is to be made, time depth must be established for all material studied, and such workers must become aware of other information on migration of peoples within New Zealand, such as is obtained from tradition, from archaeological studies and other forms of evidence. The answers are a long way off.

What these slight differences may be suggesting, then, is the possibility of multiple settlement of New Zealand, but always out of eastern Polynesia. Within this area, as we have just said, the people are so similar in appearance and culture that it is small wonder that the unravelling of New Zealand prehistory has a long way to go.

Before leaving physical differences and relationships in Polynesia there is the matter of round heads and long heads, or the relationship of cranial length to cranial breadth, a matter that has mesmerized generations of workers in the arcane realms of craniology.

The relationship between the two measurements is expressed as an index (*Fig. 5.8*).

$$\text{cranial index} \quad = \quad \frac{\text{breadth of cranium}}{\text{length of cranium}}$$

The heads of mankind range from very long (an index of about seventy) to very round (an index of about ninety). Sonorous names are attached to these forms, dolichocephalic, mesaticephalic, brachiocephalic . . . In the past, great weight has been attached to the cranial index in tracing relationships and origins of peoples. Polynesia has been thus described:

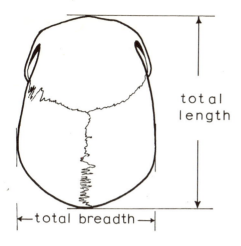

total
length

←total breadth→

Fig. 5.8: *The cranial or cephalic index, hallowed by tradition; breadth of cranium upon length of cranium.*

If the more variable traits are examined by geographic distribution, it is possible to discern a well defined pattern only in the head length, head width, and cephalic index. The Society Islands in Central Polynesia stand out as an area of marked brachycephaly, delimited by Hawaii in the north and by the neighbouring islands of the north-western Tuamotus, the Australs, and by some of the Cook Islands. Beyond this region of relative broad-headedness, central in position except for its northward extension to Hawaii, lies an encircling fringe of islands — Samoa, Tonga, the Marquesas, Mangaia, Manihiki, Rakahanga, and the Central Tuamotus — in which the cephalic index drops to levels ranging from 79 to 81. In the islands still further removed from the Society group — the south-eastern Tuamotus, Mangareva, and New Zealand — the cephalic index sinks below the upper limit of dolichoceph-aly. And finally, in the most remote eastern outposts of Polynesia, in Napuka, and Easter Island, the index reaches the lowest level for the entire area — 74·27 and 74·61, respectively. Thus, the cephalic index becomes increasingly lower as one moves from the central area and reaches its minimum on the most marginal eastern fringe. Similarly, in equivalent stages, the head length increases and the head width decreases from the Society Islands outward. It is extremely unlikely that deviations arranged in this fashion are sporadic. Such a pattern of geographic variation removes these cephalic deviations from the realm of chance and deposits them within a frame of meaning.

Within New Zealand, Scott comments:

> If any further proof were needed of the mixed origin of the Maori race it is given in this paper. An examination of the cranial indices and of the extent of their variation shows this clearly. These demonstrate two distinct types and intermediate forms. At the one extreme we have skulls approaching the Melanesian form, as met with in the Fiji group, long and narrow . . . At the other are skulls of the Polynesian type, such as are common in Tonga and Samoa, shorter and broader . . . And it must be noted that these extreme forms do not belong to different tribes or districts, but may both be found in one. Among the skulls of the Ngaitahu Tribe alone we have as great a variation . . . as is met within the entire collection of crania gathered together from all parts of both these Islands.

Scott regarded longheads as being typical of Melanesians, and considered their mingling with round heads in New Zealand to be indicative of an origin from the two racial stocks. An alternative view would be that such a mingling indicates that the cranial vault is a very plastic and variable thing and that variations in the cranial index have not much meaning. This would be a more recent view, with much experimental support, and with the Polynesian the consistency of the other major and distinctive skull features throughout makes the variations in cranial index look rather trivial.

One attempt to make sense of long heads and round heads has been the suggestion that long heads are typical of races living in hot climates where the larger surface area of the head maximises heat loss: whereas the round head, possessing a smaller surface area, is a cold climate characteristic, for preservation of body heat. The Polynesian evidence does not support this notion.

To summarize the study of relations, within and beyond Polynesia, as determined by the skeletal record — which is far from adequate. We need at present trace our first Polynesians no further than somewhere close to the western margin of the Polynesian triangle, if we agree that they define themselves by bodily form. From a very limited gene pool the founding group spread slowly eastward, then north and south to the limits of the triangle. Relationships within the triangle follow the time chart of settlement. The specific island origin (or origins) of the New Zealanders has not yet been defined, but lies in central eastern

Polynesia. We cannot yet be sure whether New Zealand was reached by only one, or several groups spread over centuries. There is slight evidence that the East Coast and central North Island peoples are a little different from others. If the latter they all came out of eastern Polynesia. Within New Zealand, including the Chathams, the striking thing is the physical similarity of the people through one thousand years of prehistory, and there is no evidence of anything other than Polynesian genes.

Table 5.1

Similarity of various words amongst the languages of Polynesia. The consonants change, or are dropped, the vowels remain the same.

LOCALITY	CANOE	HOUSE	SKY	BOWL	BELOW
New Zealand	waka	whare	rangi	kumete	raro
Cook Islands	vaka	'are	rangi	kumete	raro
Society Islands	va'a	fare	ra'i	'umete	raro
Marquesas	vaka	fare	ragi	kumete	'a'o
Mangareva	vaka	'are	ragi	kumete	raro
Hawaii	wa'a	hale	lani	'umeke	lalo
Samoa	va'a	fale	lagi	'umete	lalo
Tonga	vaka	fale	lagi	kumete	lalo

6. Life Span, Fertility and Population

The crew of that first canoe to gouge tracks up a New Zealand beach must have gazed around with awe — amongst all their other emotions — at the vast and endless land. Coast and hills ran on for ever, and nothing in memory or tradition could have prepared them for it. New Zealand is many times larger than all the other islands of Polynesia put together, and one hundred and fifty generations in the Pacific would scarcely have taken them back to a land mass as big, New Guinea or the coast of Asia.

Certainly much of this new home, they quickly learned, was taken up by barely-habitable hills and uninhabitable mountains — convenient places for gods — yet there remained a cornucopia of coast and lower land to exploit. If in the beginning there was much to learn about the new environment and the winning of food from it, at least in places there was protein striding the landscape in massive, packaged form, large flightless birds that had never seen man. As an animal increases in size its body volume increases disproportionately, and it is economic of human energy to be able to deal with large animals — provided they are not too ferocious. And if this new land was not the tropical Pacific, neither was the climate as brisk as today. A number of studies, of changes in vegetation, of tree rings, of lichen growth, of changes in the levels of glaciers, and other physical and biological evidence suggest that the climate ten centuries ago was slightly warmer and New Zealand generally had more settled weather. So initially some of the tropical food plants could be successfully grown a little further south than today. Although this is not the place to discuss it, it seems that this more favourable climate declined in the seventeenth century, and had a significant impact on New Zealand's prehistory.

These first settlers multiplied to reach a population estimated by Cook at one hundred thousand, a figure not much exceeded by most later thoughtful calculations. The intriguing question is, how few could there have been of those discoverers, standing there on some pohutakawa-fringed beach, searching apprehensively around with their eyes? How few could there have been for them to survive and multiply and succeed? While they might have been reinforced once, twice, several times, the evidence for this is still, as we know, inconclusive. Could a single canoe-load have occupied the land, expanding in, say, one thousand years, to the population Cook found?

This is not the place to debate the *why* of the matter, and the argument, accident or design, deliberate, informed voyaging or accidental drift, is likely to be tossed around till the end of time without any consensus being reached. But two points may be noted. Firstly, generation after generation after generation brought up on narrow craft a few inches above the sea will read it in a manner no modern man can hope to emulate. In this regard, the modern master mariner is little closer to the sea than the armchair theoretician. And secondly, these accidents occurred time and time and time again, over millennia, in the history of the Pacific, and repeatedly with a curiously well-equipped stock of the essentials for starting again — a varied and fertile array of plants and animals. The pigs and the chickens finally got left behind in eastern Polynesia, not much else.

How many came? Could it have been as few as one canoe load? Modern computer-based studies can throw light on these questions. There is nothing magical about the computer, no esoteric thought-processes are involved, but it does enable various data to be paired and compared in a vast number of combinations, and the likelihood of any particular event determined. The conclusions depend entirely, not on the computer, but on the validity of the assumptions fed into it. In the present situation the computer is provided with various estimates of the vital statistics of early populations, particularly those relating to birth rates and death rates. The chances of survival of any small group are calculated and, if it survives, its subsequent rate of growth. One source of these statistics may be studies of recent people still living a tribal existence, though such people are rapidly disappearing through assimilation and disease. Still, good studies have been made from regions as diverse as the Kalahari, Northern Australia, the New Guinea Highlands and the Amazon Basin. To this information we add that gleaned from the remains of populations long dead. These are the basic data, and unless they are meticulously and accurately obtained, all the glamour of the computer and its conclusions are only error. To anticipate, these data are really rather startling to those brought up in the West in the last generation or so. We have very quickly, all too quickly, forgotten what life has been like for man during most of his lifetime on the planet. We accept, and expect, an average life span exceeding seventy years, and a man dying in his fifties is regarded as being cut off in his prime. We assume that without contraception women will inevitably bear child after child, six, eight, ten in a

83

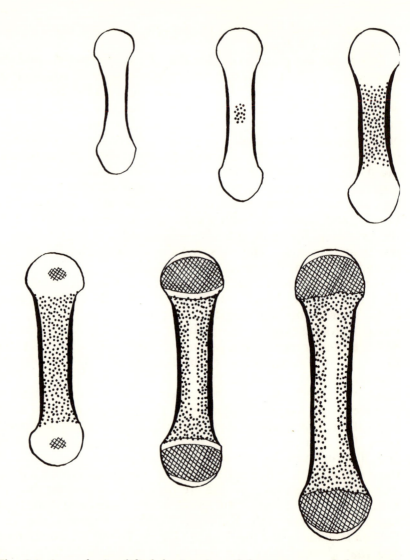

Fig. 6.1: *A much-simplified depictation of the sequence of changes in the growth of a typical long bone of the skeleton. A purely cartilaginous precursor of the bone develops, within its shaft during fetal life, a primary centre of bone (stippled in the diagram). This gradually extends up and down the shaft of the bone. Quite soon after birth secondary centres of bone appear at the ends (cross-hatched in the diagram). Until growth ceases in the late teens or early twenties these secondary centres remain separated from the primary centre by a plate of cartilage, the growth plate. The fairly set order of fusion of primary with secondary centres allows accurate ageing of individuals under the age of about twenty-five years.*

reproductive lifetime. Chronic illness and prolonged pain are unknown to most of us.

The past tells a very different story, and to read it we must assemble data on these matters of length of life, and fertility and childbearing in prehistory. Only then can some judgement be made on the numbers required to initially settle New Zealand if a population of say one hundred and twenty-five thousand was to be reached in the present estimate of one thousand years of human prehistory. Such data comes from some basic biological observations.

Bones develop and grow and allow accurate assessment of age, particularly up to about twenty-five years. Most bones of the body appear before birth, being formed from one or more primary centres. To allow continued growth through childhood the bones develop secondary centres or epiphyses in early childhood, which are separated from the primary centre by a layer of growth cartilage (*Fig. 6.1*). As adult dimensions are attained and growth ceases, the epiphyses fuse with the primary centre and the growth cartilage is obliterated. There is a fairly set and organized 'flow' of epiphyseal appearance and fusion, and it is a knowledge of this pattern that enables an estimate of the age of a younger person from prehistory to be made. First appearance of epiphyses is not usually of much use in prehistoric studies as they start as unidentifiable (in location) marbles of bone which become displaced with the centuries in the ground. But from the later period of childhood their shape is more like that of the final bone end and they are recognizable and gradually become attached to the main part of the bone (*Figs. 6.2* and *6.3*). Assessment of later epiphyseal development and fusion is one of the most accurate and easiest ways of ageing human material. Fusion reaches its maximum between the ages of about sixteen and twenty years. Thereafter, there are not very many left to fuse and increasingly it is only possible to comment from this aspect that the individual was 'adult' or 'mature'. One of the last epiphyses to fuse is at the inner end of the clavicle or collar bone, which joins up with the main bone at about twenty-six years. Other bony indicators, not strictly epiphyses, are the various segments of the sacrum, of which the upper joins (erratically) with the second at about thirty years (*Fig. 6.4*), and a joint in the base of the cranium between the sphenoid and occipital bones that closes by about twenty-two years.

The teeth, like the bones, develop and grow, and as their enamel is the hardest substance in the body, with the dentine not much behind, they also have the advantage of often outlasting

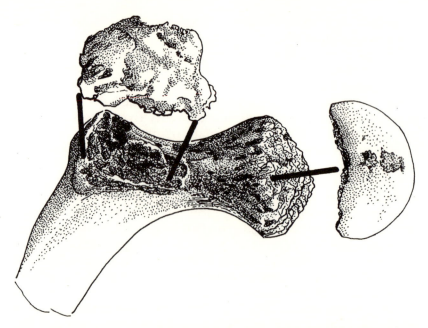

Fig. 6.2: *The upper end of the femur (thigh bone) has two secondary centres that join with the main bone at about 16 years of age.*

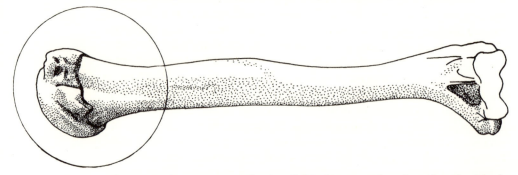

Fig. 6.3: *The upper epiphysis of this humerus has just fused with the shaft, but a groove is still clearly visible. The lower end fused about five years earlier. This individual would have been about 20 years old.*

other evidence. Bone may be crumbling and useless for ageing when a few teeth may still tell the story clearly. Particularly in children does tooth development offer a fairly precise guide to age.

The basic structure of a tooth is shown in *Fig. 6.5*. The teeth develop, as everyone knows, in two sets: firstly the milk dentition of twenty teeth, which lasts for about the first twelve years of life.

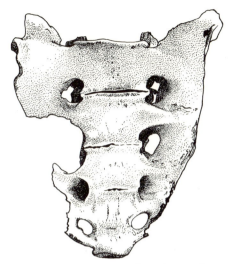

Fig. 6.4: *The upper segments of the sacrum often do not fuse until late in the third decade of life.*

The permanent teeth gradually appear during childhood and the milk teeth are eventually lost. This pattern of formation and eruption of the teeth differs somewhat between races. In general, European children have later times of eruption for individual teeth than do children of Polynesian, Negro or Asiatic ancestry. One study showed the upper canines of Polynesian boys to erupt fully two years before those of European boys. This is an extreme example and the numbers in this particular study were not large, but one must be aware that a Polynesian child will be younger than his European counterpart with a similar dentition. Nutrition also affects time of tooth eruption to a slight extent.

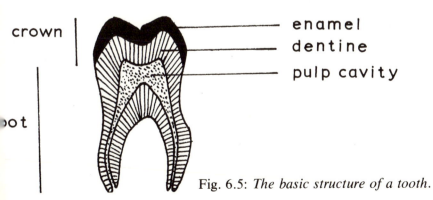

crown

root

enamel
dentine
pulp cavity

Fig. 6.5: *The basic structure of a tooth.*

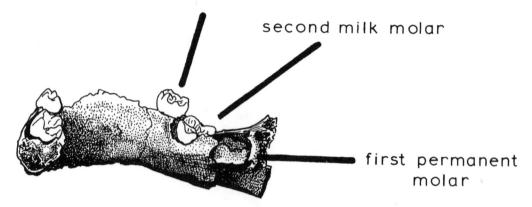

first milk molar

second milk molar

first permanent molar

Fig. 6.6: *Part of an infant's mandible (lower jaw) illustrating the value of tooth eruption in ageing. On both sides the first milk molar has erupted and the second milk molar is just emerging from the bone. On the right side the first permanent molar can be seen forming in the depths of the bone. The estimated age is about 20 months.*

The enamel crowns of the milk teeth are formed within the bone of the jaw before birth. After birth they erupt at fairly consistent intervals and in a well defined order. As every parent knows, the lower central incisors are first to appear at about six months, and are followed by the upper central incisors. Thereafter, the other incisors, molars and canines successively merge, the last being the second molar which appears at about two years of age (*Fig. 6.6*). At this stage, even when the crown of a tooth is clearly visible and fully erupted, its root is still immature. A further period of some months must elapse before the root is fully grown. This state of root development may be assessed by X-rays, or in skeletal material by direct examination if the teeth are loose (*Fig. 6.7*). Up to the age of two years, age can therefore be accurately judged by the 'flow', or eruption and development of the milk teeth.

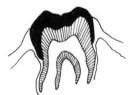

Fig. 6.7: *After the crown of a tooth is complete the degree of formation of the root may still give an indication of age. Here, on the right the roots of a tooth are still widely open at their ends, though the tooth would have erupted above the gum. On the left the tooth is shown in cross-section (compare with Fig. 6.5).*

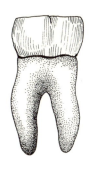

Fig. 6.8: *The blunting of tooth roots with age. The tooth on the left belonged to a 20-year-old, that on the right to a 30-year-old.*

Between the ages of two and six years the completion of development of the second milk molar root, and then the gradual formation of the first permanent molar in the depths of the bone behind it, may be observed with X-rays.

From six years onwards comes the 'flow' of the permanent dentition, and in the same way the order of eruption and of root development allows an accurate assessment of age. The easiest figures to remember are the times of eruption of the three permanent molars, at six, twelve, and eighteen years. These are round figures, and there must be a range of eruption times, but they are sufficiently accurate for many analyses. Even after the eruption of the third molar, the maturation of its root allows the age estimate to be carried through to about twenty years. The final feature in the maturation of the root, once it has reached the correct length, is a narrowing of the canal that carries nerves and blood vessels into the pulp cavity. This gradually diminishes in size until it is no longer clearly visible to the naked eye.

After about twenty years the teeth do not entirely lose their value as indicators of age. They may cease to develop, but biological processes continue, and these, like the changes in skin and bone and all the body, we can term 'ageing'. There are a number of features to note. The fully developed roots of a young adult's teeth are quite sharp. With time — from about twenty-five years on — these roots become rounded and blunter as more cement is deposited around them to cope with the varied strains thrown on the teeth. By age of thirty-five or forty they present a very different appearance from the sharper, more youthful root (*Fig. 6.8*).

The teeth wear down with age, and provided the rate of wear for a particular population can be assessed for some individuals in the population from other criteria, the remainder of the population who are represented adequately by teeth may be aged. This method of ageing by tooth wear has proved reliable on modern populations and on skeletal series of known age, and is one of the most valuable methods of ageing adults in New Zealand, where bone preservation is often poor. But the criteria of wear with age must be developed separately for each population and it would be completely misleading to apply tooth wear criteria from, for example, a tropical Pacific population, Polynesian or otherwise, to a population from New Zealand's later prehistoric period. The method would be inaccurate on a modern Western population, where there are likely to be considerable variations in diet, in dental care, and in tooth loss. The modern populations on which the method has been tested have been from less developed societies where constancy of diet and dental care (if any) exists. This points up another general fact, that it is more valid to consider the features of an individual from prehistory as being representative of his group, with its limited range of environmental exploitation, than any modern Western individual would be representative of his group. From a few prehistoric teeth one can validly make several deductions about the society in which the individual lived. To do the same with a modern individual might lead to some hilarious conclusions.

There are still other hints of age in older teeth. The pulp cavity may become filled in by dentine to some extent, and the root, for some structural reasons, gradually becomes translucent, this translucency spreading up from the tip. All these features are valuable in ageing older adults, for it is here the other, easier criteria of bone and tooth development are no longer available.

Sometimes no teeth are found, and if the remains are old and fragmentary, the search for some criterion of age then becomes a bit desperate. Fortunately there are still other skeletal indicators to turn to. One method of assessing the age of mature adults is by the changes occurring at the pubic symphysis, the joint uniting the two halves of the pelvis at the front. Some fifty years ago the anatomist Wingate Todd, British by origin and American by adoption, described the sequences of changes with age at this joint in males. In the past two decades his criteria have been revised, and criteria for females established as well. In the broadest terms, the changes involve an obliteration of the transverse grooves on the joint surfaces with increasing age, accompanied by an increasing lipping at the joint margin (*Fig. 6.9*). One reason for these changes being better known in males

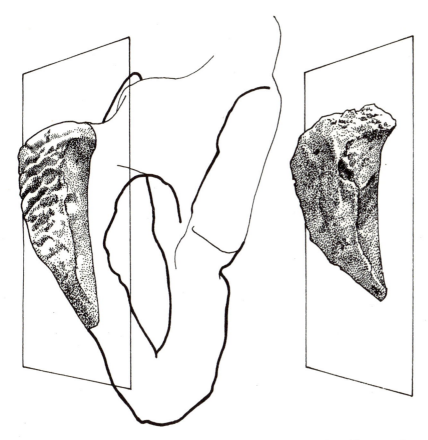

Fig. 6.9: *Age changes at the pubic joint: most noticeable are the horizontal ridges in the younger specimen on the left. These have disappeared in the older specimen on the right.*

than females is that wartime provides the most material for study — that is, more males than females are killed. Plastic casts of the joint surfaces, showing the sequence of changes, are available and allow a fairly objective assessment. Overall, the method is reasonably accurate, though past the age of thirty one can do no better than place an individual within a decade, giving the age as, say, between thirty-five and forty-five, or fifty and sixty years.

The pubic region of the pelvis is fairly fragile and does not last particularly well in the ground. Even if still present in excavated material the bone surface may be so eroded that assessment is impossible. So it may be necessary to look further for other hints of the age of an adult.

One method which has been extensively used since the last

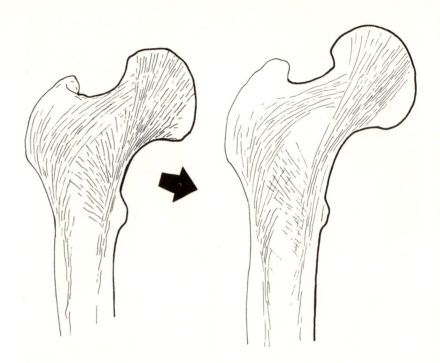

Fig. 6.10: *Showing the thinning of bone with age that occurs in the upper femur (sketched from an X-ray).*

century is the rate of fusion — that is, closure or obliteration — of the sutures of the vault of the cranium. Unfortunately, recent studies have shown the error in this method to be unacceptably large — when the error becomes so great that the possible age can only be given within a range of twenty years it is more worthwhile to make the assessment, or guess, from other bits of information. It is said that slightly greater accuracy is obtained if the suture fusion is assessed from the inner aspect of the cranium than from the outer, but all in all it is probably a method to be ignored.

As one becomes familiar with the skeletal changes in a particular group of prehistoric people it is possible, having established the ages of some adults by the more specific criteria, to make age estimates from the degree of 'wear' that the skeleton shows: that is, the pattern and degree of arthritis in the joints, and the extent of degeneration of the spine. This is a more subjective form of assessment, but when taken with other clues, such as rounding of the roots of the teeth, it is helpful in placing people within a decade. A further supplementary source of information is that obtained from X-rays of the long bones. With age there occurs in the adult a normal reduction in the thickness of the cortical bone, and in the trabeculae of the spongy bone. Changes in trabecular pattern can be particularly well seen in the upper end of the femur (*Fig. 6.10*). Judged with caution, along with all the other clues, it is a useful additional method.

It can be seen that ageing of mature adults by gross appearances lacks the accuracy possible in the younger age groups, and with incomplete and fragmentary remains may sometimes seem little more than inspired guesswork. However, there is one final method to which one can turn, and that is to the picture seen when a thin section of bone is studied under the microscope. The basic architecture of human bone has been outlined earlier. The pattern is not identical throughout life, but shows distinct and measurable changes with age. Some of these changes are shown in *Fig. 6.11*. Young bone — say from a twenty-year adult — shows circumferential rings of bone, and a relatively small number of osteons which are large in size and have wide central canals. With age the circumferential rings disappear, more and smaller osteons are formed and their central canals become smaller. These age changes can be set out fairly precisely, and the method is one of the most valuable for age estimates in adult material. It allows an age estimate to be made even on a solitary fragment of a long bone. There is a drawback, very relevant to the New Zealand situation — the bone must be in fairly good condition, its internal microscope structure being reasonably well preserved and recognizable. Now, New Zealand soils are not kind to bone, in general

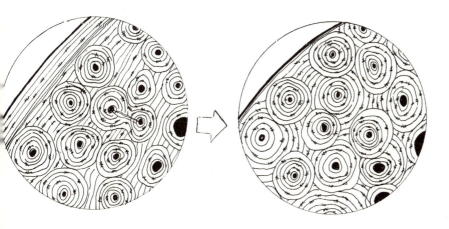

Fig. 6.11: *Microscopic changes with age in bone. The circular osteons become more numerous and extend to the outer edge of the bone.*

preservation is not good, and material dating to the earliest settlement period is often difficult to assess by this method.

Table 6.1 summarises the methods available for ageing human skeletal material, their age range and their accuracy. In practical terms tooth wear is the quickest way of assessing mature adult age in New Zealand material, with the important proviso that the date of the population be known approximately.

The application of these various methods of age assessment to a prehistoric population is well illustrated by a study of the people of Wairau Bar. This famous and well-documented early New Zealand site was excavated principally by Roger Duff of the Canterbury Museum in the 1940s and 50s, and is described in his book *The Moa Hunter Period of Maori Culture*. More than forty individuals have been scientifically examined from this site, which, on the evidence of carbon-14 dating, and nitrogen analysis of bone, was occupied from about AD 1150 through to AD 1450. While the individuals cover the entire time of settlement, there is no evidence that physical existence, diet, or genes, varied significantly over the three hundred years.

As with so much New Zealand material, particularly of such age, the remains are incomplete, fragmented and poorly preserved — the soil of the Wairau Bar is not favourable for the preservation of bone. Knowing the reputation of Cook Strait for weather one may reasonably ask whether Wairau Bar was suitable for the preservation of life itself in those prehistoric times. However, given the likely climatic changes, this now wind-swept strip of land with its covering of tussock and matagouri was probably a more kindly place, with the sea in front and the great lagoon behind to offer all the food resources necessary for survival, and even comfort.

The remains consist largely of fragments of skull with, fortunately, the majority of individuals having a considerable number of teeth still surviving. Only four or five individuals are reasonably complete. All are adults — that is over about sixteen years of age. The remains of children and infants are much more friable and the two encountered were but scarcely-discernible patterns in the ground.

The complete individuals are mature adults whose bone is unsuitable for microscopic study and who cannot accurately be aged alone. At first sight, the problem of establishing the ages of the series looked very difficult and unlikely to be satisfactorily solved. But in an analysis of the material, two small but important features came to light. Fragments of bone showed that one individual had an unfused joint between the sphenoid and occipital bones at the base of the skull. In addition, this individual showed evidence on the bone of the lower jaw that a missing third molar had erupted but that the root had not been fully formed. From this data it was reasonable to assign an age of about nineteen years to this person.

Amongst the fragmentary remains of a second individual was a third molar tooth that showed root development almost complete, but with a canal opening still not reduced to the barely perceptible mature size. This individual could be given an age of about twenty years.

These two individuals fortunately possessed reasonably complete sets of teeth. The degree of wear was, as one would hope and expect, similar between them. Ageing of the remaining twenty or more individuals proceeded as follows.

The first molar tooth on a nineteen year old has been subjected to thirteen years of wear, for it erupts at six years. If a second molar on another individual from the same population shows a similar degree of wear it can be assumed to have been exposed to a slightly longer period of wear, as it is used rather less than the first molar in chewing — say fourteen years or fifteen years. The second molar erupts at twelve years of age. Therefore, an individual with a second molar showing the same degree of wear as a nineteen year old's first molar will be aged twelve + fourteen years = twenty-six years.

In a similar way the age of an individual showing third molar wear equivalent to that of a nineteen year old's first molar will be eighteen + fourteen years = thirty-two years. In practice third molars in Polynesians tend to be absent, poorly-formed, or do not occlude, but fortunately in the Wairau Bar people full development and occlusion of third molars frequently occurred.

From this method of ageing by tooth wear — which, it is emphasized, has been shown in studies of known material, living and historic, to be reliable — it was possible to estimate the ages of the majority of the people of Wairau Bar.

A number lacked teeth, and some of the other ageing methods had to be resorted to. The degree of arthritis and spinal degeneration was of some value, and X-ray assessment of the trabecular pattern in the upper end of the femur was used in several individuals. In the end a graph showing the life span of the people of Wairau Bar could be drawn (*Fig. 6.12*).

The results, to those accustomed to the biblical adage and to modern life spans, are startling. The average age of death of these adults — adults only, with no children to drag the figures down — was twenty-eight years for the men and twenty-nine years for the

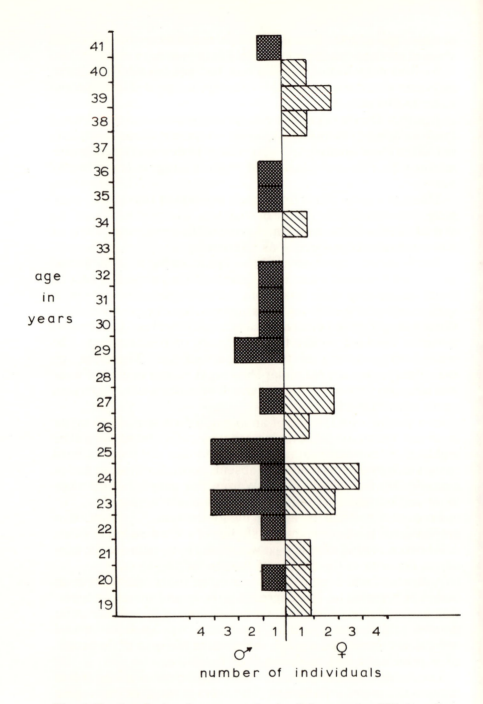

Fig. 6.12: *Graph showing age at death of the people of Wairau Bar: males to the left of the centre line and females to the right.*

women. The oldest individual barely reached into the forties, while there is a clustering of deaths in the early twenties.

Startling though these findings may be, they are fairly typical of the country as a whole. All the time, in the small populations from Motutapu Island, from Opito, from Castlepoint, from Kaikoura and coastal Otago, we find we are dealing with what nowadays would be termed 'young' adults. The oldest individuals reach into the fifties, perhaps the rare sixty, the majority die by their late twenties. I would estimate that the average age at death for the country as a whole, in the prehistoric, was a little higher than that revealed at Wairau Bar — perhaps thirty-one or thirty-two years of age.

While it would be fascinating to go back through time and assess the real accuracy of the figures, there yet seems little doubt of their validity. The results by the various methods, where they can be applied to the same individual, are in harmony — tooth wear and development, epiphyseal fusion, changes at the pubic symphysis, and the microscopic appearance, all give the same story. Very seldom is there any inconsistency.

When we look further afield the picture is repeated. In prehistoric societies generally, in the Americas, in Europe, in Asia, the average age of the adults at death is around thirty years. And not just in the prehistoric — the pattern of health and disease as revealed in the historical record suggests that right up to the present century the average life span was little better. Certainly in the West there are plenty of records of older, healthy people, plenty of older writers giving evidence of themselves, but these came inevitably from the better-fed, better-housed, more fortunate classes and cannot be considered representative of the mass of the population to which they belong. For most of mankind, for most of our time on this planet, life has been, if not the Hobbesian brutish and nasty, at least short by modern Western standards.

More will be said later about age at death in relation to activities during life. But one point should be made. The early European voyagers — Cook for example — commented on the number of older yet healthy and agile people amongst the New Zealanders. Some recent studies of tribal peoples living in favourable environments, have also commented on such older people — apparently well-preserved seventy-year-olds. In some instances it has been possible to obtain the ages of these individuals from the records of the Mission Stations where they have been born. Then they usually prove to be in their forties. I suggest that Cook's agile old people were in that same decade of life. Certainly in our studies we have not yet encountered any individual whom I would place as much over sixty years of age.

The implications of this short life span on small population groups in prehistory are considerable. The effects on health and disease patterns we will come to later. Others lie largely outside the realms of mere biological anthropology, and one can here only hint at some possibilities. Great cohesion of the group was necessary — when so many parents die young, all must be parents of a sort, and perhaps here lies the basis of the extended family pattern. In another direction, there is the possibility of rapid culture change — the apprentice can develop his individuality when the master is not looking over his shoulder for too long — and we know that culture change was indeed rapid in prehistoric New Zealand. And the *kaumatua,* the elders of the group — these would have reached the venerable age of some thirty-five years.

This sort of information on longevity can be elaborated into life tables, age-specific death rates, and other statistical forms suitable for the study of population, of demography, but only if the date is adequate. In New Zealand our information cannot support such treatment at present. Above all, localized large skeletal series do not exist. The forty individuals from Wairau Bar cover three centuries and contain not a single child or infant — not a sound basis for extending the calculations. The problem is not confined to New Zealand, for world-wide the number of localized prehistoric populations, comprehensive in age groups over extended time, and capable of providing valid data to compare with the details obtainable from modern populations, are probably no more than half a dozen. But the picture comes through. Life was short. A number of consequences follow.

This short life span is one of the factors to be considered when attempting to estimate how many need have originally arrived in New Zealand to allow survival of the group. The other dominant factor is the possible rate of replacement of these short-lived people — the fertility and fecundity of the women. Again, the picture is vastly different from that in the modern Western world. Western woman now puts a great deal of time and thought, not to say anxiety, into the business of restricting her pregnancies. Having borne two children, she may reasonably expect them to survive her. Having delivered them she faces the prospect of perhaps another thirty years of fertility which has somehow to be suppressed, in addition to a monthly period that is, at best, a nuisance. The complaint that whoever designed the system made a bad job of it might seem justified. But the answer is that the system was not designed for such artificial conditions.

Studies of tribal peoples in some of the areas already mentioned and some groups in other parts of the world, suggest that the age of menarche or onset of periods is greatly influenced by the standard of nutrition. When food is not always abundant, when perhaps there are periods of seasonal shortage, or deficiencies in some dietary components, menarche occurs at about seventeen years of age. It is clear from various historical records that this was also about the time of onset in Europe until this century. With improved nutrition and without seasonal shortages the age of menarche had dropped steadily in the Western world, until now, in most such countries, it appears to have stabilised at about thirteen years. So just by being able to live well, modern woman has added four years of problems to her life.

It is known that on average about two years of periods occur before ovulation commences. That is to say, for about two years after periods start, pregnancy cannot occur. In modern Western woman ovulation will start at about fifteen years. In a less favourable environment the possibilities of pregnancy may be delayed till about nineteen years, and this has probably been the situation for most of womankind during most of our existence on earth. (As one authority has succinctly put it, the possibility of child-bearing, and the attainment of mental maturity have, until recently, occurred at about the same time in the life of a woman. Now, for the first time in the history of the race, child-bearing may be possible well in advance of full adulthood, and to talk of teenage pregnancies as being indicative of increasing moral degradation, whatever that means, is to miss entirely the biological facts.)

Following birth a child would be breastfed, both in recent tribal societies and for most of mankind throughout history. This breastfeeding would be on demand, and recurrent, for some two years after birth. In general terms, lactation, with its accompanying suppression of periods, is a fairly effective contraceptive, suppressing ovulation by some central control. This indeed has been the major method of contraception for womankind over millennia. While medical students are taught that for the lactating mother to ignore other methods of contraception is a good way of ensuring another pregnancy, this only arises from emphasis on the individual, and modern breastfeeding tends to be less complete, less persistent, less on demand than in the tribal state, with supplementary feeding creeping in. For these reasons the suppression of ovulation may be less reliable. The lactational demands are not those of earlier times.

If a child is fully breast-fed for at least two years after birth, conception is unlikely to occur in the mother until the third year after the last child, and probably, with the added effect of sub-optimal nutrition, the average spacing between children is about four years. So, from being a creature bearing two children and then facing perhaps thirty fertile years, earlier woman became fertile later, and bore children at perhaps four-yearly intervals. We have already noted the short life span of tribal people, and if we accept an average age at death of thirty-one years for the women of prehistoric New Zealand, the number of children borne is likely to be no more than four, and perhaps three is the more likely number. In her twelve years of reproductive life she would have endured perhaps three with periods, for lactation also suppresses menstruation, and of course she would most probably have seen some of her children die. This is the 'natural' picture, and it is a long way from there to the modern Western situation.

This picture of the reproductive life of woman emerges from the study of recent tribal populations. From the past there is the skeletal evidence. What form does this evidence take and how does it agree?

Some years ago the American physical anthropologist T. D. Stewart, while modifying Wingate Todd's ageing criteria for the pubic symphysis, noted that the female symphysis was frequently distorted — and the age assessment interfered with — by a pitting of the back of the pubic bone. He came to the conclusion that these pits must be a consequence of pregnancy and child-bearing, and ascribed their immediate cause to a tearing and rupturing of the joint ligaments during childbirth.

The pits are smooth and often quite deep, and rather like the appearance of the crater formed by a raindrop in soft mud (*Fig. 6.13*). The explanation of their formation by a simple tearing and rupture of ligaments does not quite fit this smooth-walled appearance. It seems that the process is rather more prolonged, and is related to a softening and loosening of the ligaments over the last few months of pregnancy, so that the pelvis can open up slightly yet significantly during birth. This softening is caused by a hormone — appropriately called relaxin — released by the ovary. If a microscopic section is made of the attachments of these ligaments in the later months of pregnancy, large cells can be seen eroding away the bone, and creating the pits. When these pits are found they are, obviously, conclusive evidence of the sex of the individual. They survive for many years, probably never being completely obliterated.

The other joints of the pelvis which have to open up during

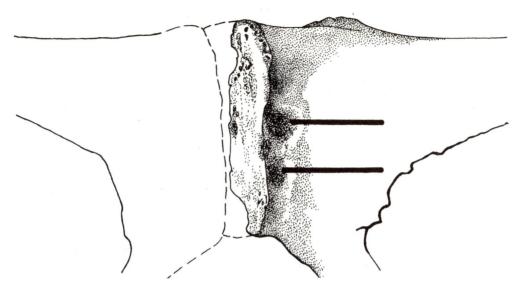

Fig. 6.13: *The lines indicate pits of pregnancy on the back of the pubic bone.*

child-birth are at the back, between the hip bone on each side and the sacrum. It would be logical to expect these joints to be under the influence of the hormone relaxin and to show the same pitted appearance — and this is certainly the case. On the hip bone adjacent to this joint (the sacroiliac joint) is a conspicuous groove, found in both males and females, and formed by a strong ligament. In females who have borne children, this groove becomes much altered, being now formed by a succession, a line, of the same sort of pits as are found on the back of the pubic bone (*Fig. 6.14*).

This change of pregnancy in the groove at the back of the pelvis is one of the most useful sexing criteria, because the bone here is very solid, and survives well in the ground, in contrast to the more fragile pubic bone at the front, which has often disintegrated or eroded beyond recognition.

Not only is it possible to state conclusively whether or not a woman has borne children, but it is also possible to make an estimate of how many have been borne. This can be done by comparing the material with modern specimens of known parity (number of children). This sort of information, apart from often providing conclusive evidence of sex, obviously offers valuable data about a prehistoric group, their fertility, their chances of survival, and their likely rate of increase or decrease in numbers with time.

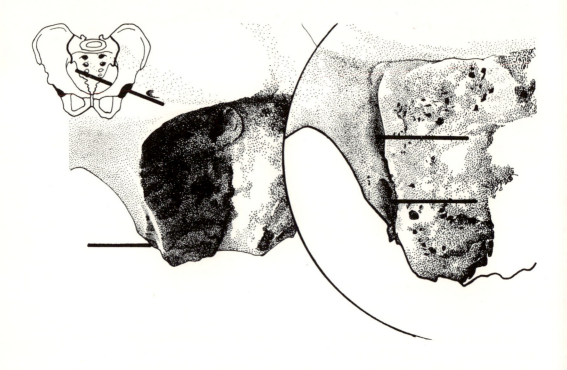

The inset explains the view, looking across, towards the back of the pelvis.

Fig. 6.14: *Ligament grooves at the back of the pelvis, where the hip bone joins the sacrum. The illustration on the left shows the groove of a male pelvis or of a female that has not been exposed to the hormonal changes of pregnancy. On the right is the 'pitted' groove of pregnancy with the pits indicated by the lines.*

Establishing the sex of human remains is one of the most basic and revealing things in these prehistoric studies. For example, it may throw light on the social structure and customs of the group being studied. If we find that the females of a group are consistently showing evidence of undernourishment and of a poorer diet, and that they are buried carelessly and with few or no burial offerings, then we can reasonably assume that females had a much lower standing than males in the social hierachy. A prehistoric Australian aboriginal burial area revealed no females in a group of over one hundred individuals, so unless there is evidence of separate burial areas for the sexes we can assume that females were not highly regarded. It can be said straight away that this is not the picture presented by the evidence of prehistoric New Zealanders. The first studies of the Wairau Bar population suggested that careful interment and rich grave goods, including moa eggs, were limited to males of high rank. But a reassessment of the material reveals that the females there were certainly buried with grave goods including moa eggs. There may be a tendency for the males to have rather the richer artefacts, but I would not think, on the present numbers, we can conclusively state this. From other parts of the country — for example the well-known burial cave on Lake Hauroko on the fringes of Fiordland — there is ample evidence that females could be accorded the same honours as males.

As we have just touched on the conclusive evidence of femininity — the imprint of pregnancy — there is place here for comment on other bony criteria of sex. The sex of children and infants cannot be reliably judged, and it is only after puberty that reasonable accuracy can be claimed. The chances of being correct are, of course, considerably better than when estimating age. Assuming custom treated male and female equally, there is a 50 percent chance of getting the sex correct and a toss of a coin would give the same overall result. But we must be more specific than that.

In assessing the sex of skeletal material the greatest accuracy is obtained from the pelvis, even without any imprint of pregnancy. This is understandable because here alone in the body are the biological requirements radically different between the sexes. The female pelvis is specifically adapted for childbearing, and a number of features may readily be distinguished from the male form. One of the easiest to interpret is the arch, or curve of the bone, under the front of the pelvis, which in the female appears as a broad, inverted U shape, in contrast to the sharper V-shaped angle of the male pelvis (*Fig. 6.15*). Another is the form of the large notch seen from the side, the sciatic notch. Again, in the female this is a more open U shape, as opposed to the narrow, straight-sided male notch. Viewed from above, the typical female pelvis has a more rounded, more capacious cavity. When all of these features are taken into account, it has been found, in studies on recent material of known sex, that about 95 percent accuracy of sexing is obtained, and no other part of the skeleton allows such accuracy.

After the pelvis, the skull is said to offer the greatest accuracy, but 'blind' tests by recognised authorities on recent series of known sex give only about 85 percent accuracy. In less expert

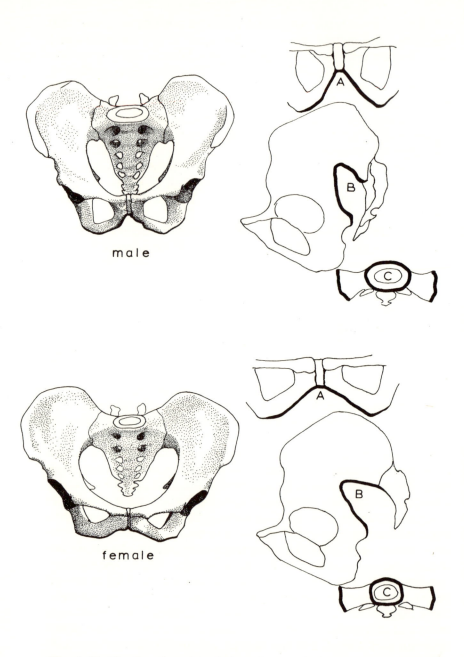

Fig. 6.15: *The female pelvis (below) has a more capacious cavity than the male (above). Some specific differences are depicted on the right: The sub-pubic arch (A) is wider in the female, as is the sciatic notch (B). The body of the sacrum (C) is broader and more robust in the male.*

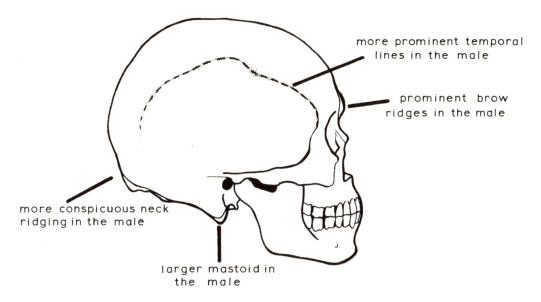

more prominent temporal
lines in the male

prominent brow
ridges in the male

more conspicuous neck
ridging in the male

larger mastoid in
the male

Fig. 6.16: *Some sex differences in the skull.*

hands the accuracy may therefore not exceed 80 percent, and this
relatively low level is a bit disturbing when one thinks of the
aplomb and confidence with which fragmentary skull remains are
assigned as male or female.

The skull features of particular value are arranged around the
margins of the vault (*Fig. 6.16*). To generalise: at the front, males
have prominent brow ridges, with rounded margins to the eye
sockets and a prominent bulge (the glabella) above the bridge of
the nose. At the side of the head the mastoid processes, behind the
ears, are large. At the back of the skull the ridges for the
attachment of the neck muscles are substantial. By contrast,
females have inconspicuous brow ridges, sharp eye socket
margins and, at the back, less conspicuous muscular markings.
But the Polynesian female head may often look very masculine —
for example the mastoid processes are frequently quite big — and
it is not uncommon to find an unequivocally female pelvis
belonging to a head that one would otherwise classify as male.

Other parts of the skeleton apart from pelvis and skull can still
offer fairly accurate evidence of sex. The male bones are
generally bigger, more robust, with more distinct muscle markings. These features can be simply assessed, subjectively, by eye,

or greater precision can be obtained by making measurements and subjecting these measurements to a particular form of statistical analysis. Theoretically, any skeletal measurement in the body could be subjected to such an analysis, but in practice one is limited to dimensions whose significance for sexing one has previously determined from a series of the same population and of known sex. Dimensions commonly used are the lengths of the major long bones of the limbs, and the teeth. The skull and the pelvis may also be sexed by these mathematical means, but, for the pelvis at least, such elaborations are pointless when assessment by eye gives high, and sometimes absolute accuracy. But where these statistical elaborations are called for, as with fragmentary, incomplete remains, they afford high accuracy (up to 90 percent of the accuracy of sexing the original series) and are a valuable method to fall back on. The major joints of the limbs also show distinct differences in dimensions between the sexes, and a single measurement, the diameter of the head of the femur, may be a very good guide. In New Zealand material a femoral head diameter of 44mm marks the boundary between most males and most females.

There still are times when the remains are so very incomplete and fragmentary that sexing by these usual gross methods is impossible, yet where, because of the specific situation, some judgment on the sex of the individual is highly desirable. Here it is possible to fall back on chemical methods. Female bone, at least between puberty and menopause, has a higher citrate level than male bone. This is related to the necessity for higher citrate reserves in the body because of certain effects of the female hormonal cycle. This difference in citrate level can be ascertained and an assignment of sex made. On present evidence the method, which is somewhat tricky and tedious to carry out, gives an accuracy as good as most other methods — about 90 percent. In the New Zealand situation where so much material is in very poor state, this citrate method, which uses only a minute amount of bone, is proving very valuable — for example, it has confirmed the sexes assigned to the fragmentary and incomplete Wairau Bar series.

Leaving this digression into sexing to return to the pelvic evidence of past pregnancy: we know that studies of recent tribal people suggest a three to four-year interval between births, and that childbearing starts at about age nineteen. We also know that the average length of life for those attaining adulthood in prehistoric New Zealand was a little more than thirty years. On this information we would anticipate the average number of children borne to prehistoric New Zealand women to be three or four.

The bony evidence does support this view. A study of female pelves from prehistoric New Zealand gave the results set out in *Fig. 6.17*. The number of children borne, as estimated from the pelvic markings, increased gradually with the age of the individuals, and only those over thirty-five years were judged to have borne four or more children. (The average age at death of these women was about thirty-five years, rather higher than one would place the overall average for prehistoric New Zealanders). It is unusual for a female pelvis from prehistory not to show markings of pregnancies — a 'natural' infertility rate of 2-3 percent is probably to be expected.

There are other facets of these matters of fertility and fecundity. In a hunter-gatherer society breastfeeding is particularly likely to be persistent and continuous for at least two years after childbearing because of a general lack of suitable foods onto which to wean a young child. With the development of agriculture such supplementary foods are more likely to be available, breastfeeding more erratic and its contraceptive effect less reliable. Perhaps for this reason many tribal societies have developed prohibitions against intercourse after childbirth, for varying periods, in order to prevent excessive growth in their numbers. With hunter-gatherer societies such growth is strictly limited by what a mother can carry — one child and some

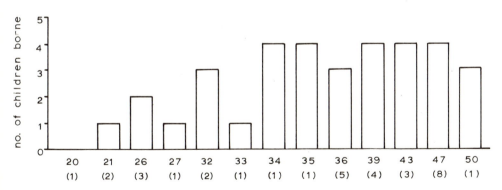

Fig. 6.17: *Results of a study of pregnancy markings in a series of prehistoric New Zealand pelves. A complete range of ages was not available, and the number in brackets under each given age is the number of individuals of that age. The graph shows a rise to a maximum of four children from age 34 onwards. These 33 women bore a total of 101 children, which is an average of just over three for each woman.*

household paraphenalia. This may be the real reason, whatever the esoteric ones, for killing of twins by Australian Aborigines. Abortion and infanticide are the obvious methods of coping with children who cannot be accommodated. L. E. Gluckman, a psychiatrist who has studied some aspects of Maori belief, quotes a number of early sources who suggest that infanticide was regularly resorted to in New Zealand, and it is recorded in other parts of Polynesia. Certainly the growing population pressures in northern New Zealand in the later prehistoric would have encouraged the practice, and there is no particular evidence of respect for individual human life. Even within New Zealand the incidence of such practices may have differed between regions and over the centuries. The south was probably more of a hunter-gatherer culture than the warmer north and had lesser population pressures.

Like the figures for life-span, these data for childbearing in prehistoric New Zealand are still inadequate in number and localization to put into modern statistical form, such as age-specific birth rates. Yet together they are sufficient to allow us to assess the validity of studies that have been made on the chances of survival and growth of small groups. One such computer study was referred to earlier. This, based on modern data from Pacific populations, suggested that as few as three males and three females in their early twenties could have an almost 50 percent chance of surviving and multiplying. Increasing the founding population to ten or fourteen young adults reduced the chances of extinction to about 20 percent. This sounds remarkably like a canoe load. As in all these computer studies, the data supplied is all-important. The study from which the data in Table 6.2 is taken probably takes the age of fertility a bit low, at fifteen years, but on the other hand in some analyses insisted on monogamy — perhaps an unlikely stricture. One assumption adds a bit of fertility, the other takes a bit away. The calculations used in the table are probably reasonable for the New Zealand situation.

The same computer study indicated the size reached by theoretical populations before they became extinct. Very few reached thirty in number and then turned round, shrank and disappeared. Once a population of fifty was reached the community would have been reasonably secure. Before that level a single canoe accident could have jeopardized everything. The calculations suggested that a level of fifty could be reached in about one hundred years — say by AD 900 in the New Zealand situation. Thereafter a growth rate of a little under 1 percent, which is small by the standards of recent tribal societies that have been studied and would seem to be well within the capabilities of this robust people, who after all had the time and energy to throw up an astonishing number of earthworks and fortifications, is all that was required to bring them to some one hundred and twenty-five thousand at the time of Cook's first voyage. Considering the evidence for early widespread settlement of the country and the profusion of earthworks in the northern part of this early period, it may be more realistic to postulate a growth rate of more than 1 percent in the early period, reducing to less than 1 percent after, say, AD 1500 as a result of many factors — a relative over-population in the face of climatic change and environmental deterioration, pressure on food resources, with warfare and infanticide. Another possibility, considering that a natural popu-lation increase of 1 percent is low by the standards of recent tribal societies that have been studied, is that New Zealand may have been settled earlier than the present estimate of about AD 800. But there is not yet any convincing evidence of this. In the end it can be suggested that a single surviving canoe-load of some half-dozen young adults, arriving about AD 800, had an almost even chance of surviving, and populating the land. Whether this was all we do not yet know, but the idea is less fanciful than some — for example the suggestion that a pregnant woman clinging to a sea-borne log could have peopled Australia. What is certain is that most of the questions are still unanswered.

Table 6.1

Some methods of ageing skeletal material

Method	Comments
tooth eruption and formation	reliable
tooth wear	reliable for a specific population
epiphyseal fusion	reliable
pubic joint changes	fairly reliable
arthritis	sometimes useful to confirm other estimates
skull suture closure	better to guess
microscopic section of bone	reliable if bone preservation is satisfactory
X-ray changes in spongy bone	useful to support estimates from other features

Table 6.2

Chances of survival for populations founded by 6, 10 and 14 persons, sexes equal, with the women aged 18-20 years and no marriage restrictions (ie: polygamy and/or incest allowed). From a computer study.

Number in founding group	Chances of survival
6	48%
10	82%
14	85%

7. Health

Information on health in the past may come from simple things, and we have already looked at some of them. Firstly there is stature. These New Zealanders, we have learned, were tall people, the men averaging more than 1700mm (five foot seven inches) in height. It seems very likely that frequently they attained their full potential height, a situation certainly not existing in Europe at the time, emerging only now in Japan, and still not found in some less fortunate parts of the world. Their stature alone indicates a generally healthy population, or at least an adequate diet throughout the growing years, and as no major differences in stature seem to exist between various parts of the country it is probable that diet was usually adequate throughout, however it might have varied in content. However it must be warned that evidence is accumulating that some communities in some eras found life harsh, and an overall generalization of good health for all may require much qualification.

But the bones are usually robust and the markings — ridges, crests and depressions — where the muscles or their tendons are attached to the bone, very prominent in both sexes. One of the most conspicuous examples is seen in the humerus, the bone of the upper arm. About half-way down on its outer side is attached the deltoid muscle, which forms the rounded bulk of the shoulder. In the prehistoric New Zealander the humerus is raised into a very conspicuous eminence at this site of attachment, so much so that bone gives the impression of being curved outwards, though in reality the shaft is straight (*Fig. 7.1*). This eminence or tuberosity exists in the humeri of other races, but seldom as pronounced in form as in these Polynesians. The development is fairly equally marked on both right and left arms, suggesting that the basis for it is overall muscularity rather than a feature acquired as a result of some activity.

X-rays make it possible to measure the thickness of the compact bone forming the shafts of the long bones. The value of this is that there are many studies on modern and earlier populations relating the cortical thickness to nutrition (particularly in childhood) and physical activity (particularly in adult life). Malnutrition in childhood leads to underdevelopment of the cortex — it is thinner. In younger adult life, an inadequate diet does not seem to be well correlated with cortical thickness — it is rather as if, having reached normal adult proportions, the bone can maintain itself even if the diet is persistently marginal. With

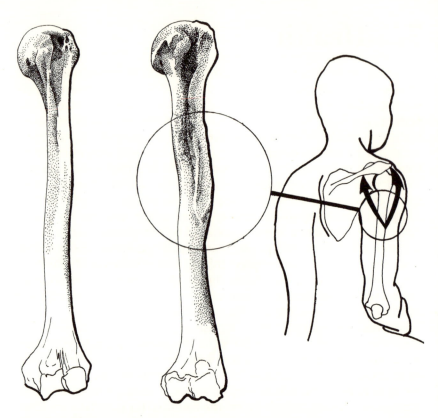

Fig. 7.1: *The muscular tuberosity on the side of the humerus (upper arm bone) is particularly well developed in the Polynesian, when compared with a non-Polynesian bone on the left. The diagram on the right shows how the deltoid muscle, which forms the roundness of the shoulder is attached to this tuberosity. The right shoulder has been drawn to best display the muscle, but the bones are from the left side.*

age, however, there is a natural thinning of the cortex. (We have seen how a similar change in the spongy bone is useful as an ageing indicator.) If physical activity is considerable, this natural thinning is warded off to some extent, occurring more slowly than in someone leading a sedentary life. In Table 7.1 are shown some figures for cortical thickness of one of the hand bones for a number of contemporary adult groups, including sedentary Americans and lusty Norwegian lumberjacks. The New Zealanders give values at the lower levels of these well-nourished moderns, which, considering that the X-rays of the former were taken on dry bone with slight shrinkage, compared to living bone with an inevitable slight contribution from the soft tissues, is probably fair evidence of the adequate nourishment of the New Zealanders.

These X-ray studies on the robustness of the Polynesian skeleton can offer other information on health, or rather, the shadowy margin between health and illness. Sometimes when a long bone is X-rayed distinct horizontal lines are seen crossing the shaft (*Fig. 7.2*). These are called 'lines of arrested growth' or Harris lines after the first investigator to comment at length on them. It seems that these lines are formed in the growing long bone (that is, before fusion of the epiphyses with the shaft) when the child or youth is subjected to an illness of some severity, or undergoes a period of malnutrition, and the growth of the bone is slowed for a period. Harris lines appear most clearly and consistently in the lower tibia, and while there is no doubt that some disappear or become less distinct with age, it is likely that once a substantial line is formed it stays as a permanent record of the event. The actual cause is said to be a slowing down of bone formation at the cartilaginous growth plate. A thicker plate of cartilage forms and this subsequently becomes converted to bone when the illness is recovered from or the diet improves. A number of studies on prehistoric, historic and modern populations suggest that in general terms the incidence of Harris lines in a population is an indicator of the general health of the population in childhood — up to at least the age of twelve years. For example, studies on modern Guatemalan children living in poor conditions have shown a high incidence of Harris lines, compared with the

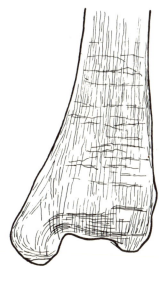

Fig. 7.2: *Lines of arrested growth are seen as rather faint horizontal lines in this sketch of an X-ray of the lower tibia (shin bone).*

minimal incidence in modern American (or New Zealand) children. In Britain a study of two adjacent early historic populations, one living on uplands, the other in apparently unhealthy swampy country, showed that the latter had a higher incidence of disease or malnutrition as judged by the Harris lines.

A review of available long bone X-rays on prehistoric New Zealanders supports the conclusion obtained from a study of stature and bone robustness — that those surviving to adult life generally had healthy childhoods and an adequate diet. And at present we can detect no clear change in this pattern with time — there seems to be no variation in physique, or in the incidence of Harris lines over the eight hundred years or so of the skeletal record, which is interesting in view of the dietary story which we will come to. (Such a conclusion may well be altered by further studies.) Some adults show a single line or a couple, but recurring lines, year after year, particularly suggesting seasonal deprivation of food, are uncommon. It is worth noting that the lines in a bone are frequently matching, that is, there is an upper and lower one, where each growth cartilage has slowed. When this occurs, the age at which the illness or episode of malnutrition occurred can be accurately assessed from the length of the shaft of the bone at the time, and even if the line is only found at one end a reasonable assessment can still be made. When the remains of children are examined they more frequently show lines of arrested growth, indications, presumably, of a decline in health and the episodes leading to death.

These X-rays signs are therefore a valuable source of information in assessing general health in the past, and support the present view that growing up in prehistoric New Zealand was generally a healthy affair. These strong, tall active adults got through childhood with a good diet and little illness. But what then starts to happen is most interesting. The bones bear evidence of extreme physical activity, and even in the first decade of adult life, between twenty and thirty years, we can note how the effect of such extreme activity starts to spill over into the realms of pathology, of disease.

When the precursors of man first started to get up on their hind legs, freeing the forelimbs for other tasks such as the fashioning of tools, unplanned-for strains were imposed on some parts of the body. Some of these parts have never managed to evolve really adequately to meet the forces imposed on them. The legacy of our four-footed past, for which we were really designed, is seen in such troubles as varicose veins, hernias (ruptures), and in the vulnerability of the spine to degeneration, to a sort of arthritis. All the upper body weight as well as any loads carried, must devolve on the spine, particularly the lower, lumbar part, and it is really not built to take such forces. Some cynical orthopaedic surgeons regard low back pain as a normal condition for mankind. The individual vertebrae are made up of spongy bone, which, as we know, naturally thins with age, and in addition the spine is required to develop a series of curves so as to keep the head balanced at the top, above the centre of gravity. When physical activity is vigorous and habitual, the spine tends to show the effects early. A number of studies of modern groups involved in weight-lifting and judo have shown the early degeneration found in prehistoric peoples.

The parts of the spine that show the highest incidence of arthritis and degeneration in these prehistoric New Zealanders are the mobile areas, the neck and the lower back. The intermediate vertebrae, to which the ribs are attached and which are less mobile, have a much lesser incidence of degeneration. The low back problems are common, often appear very early in adult life — in the early twenties — and may be extreme, with gross

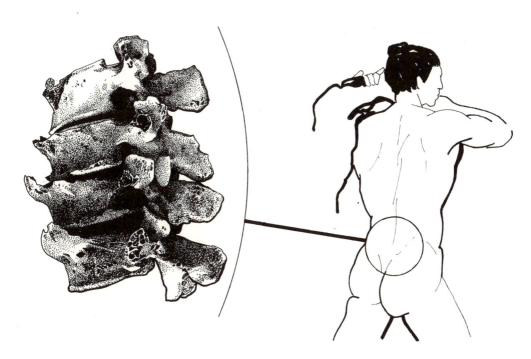

Fig 7.3: *Frequent carrying of heavy loads have led to the degenerative changes in this man's lower spine.*

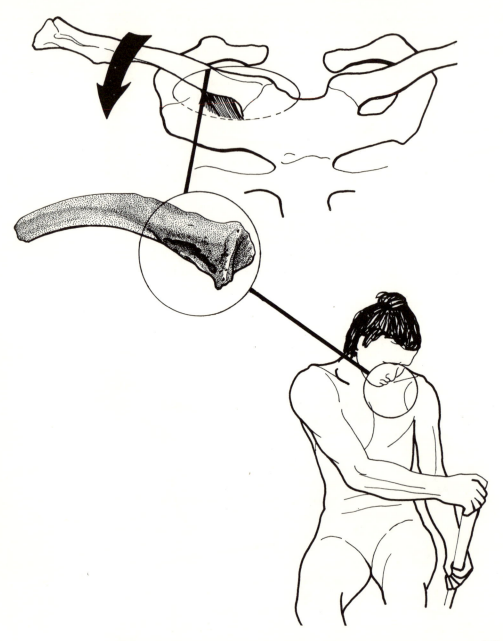

Fig. 7.4: *Vigorous downward movement of the arm, as in paddling, throws great strain on the ligament at the inner end of the collar-bone, which comes to deeply mark the bone. In addition the collar-bone becomes grooved by the first rib just outside the attachment of the ligament.*

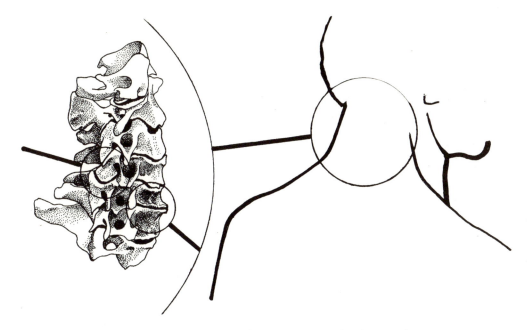

Fig. 7.5: *Prolonged and vigorous use of the arms can lead to early arthritis of the neck vertebrae. Paddling of canoes was probably the usual cause of this.*

bony lipping of the vertebrae, protrusions of the inter-vertebral disc into the bone, and flattening and collapse of the vertebrae (*Fig. 7.3*). The incidence of lower spine degeneration is usually inversely related to its incidence in the neck region and the presence of clavicular grooves. On the under-surface of the collar bone or clavicle, at its inner end, is an area for attachment of a strong ligament that binds the bone down to the cartilage of the first rib. This ligamentous area is often extremely roughened and hollowed out, indicating that it has been subject to considerable strains (*Fig. 7.4*). But the interesting feature is the occasional presence of a groove in the bone just outside this ligamentous attachment. When the anatomy of the intact skeleton is considered, it appears that this groove must be made by the clavicle being forced down on the upper surface of the first rib, a contact which can only be achieved by an extreme downward motion of the whole arm. The most likely activity that would involve such a motion seems to be paddling a canoe, where the paddle bites deeply into the water. No other activity, such as hoeing or preparing ground for planting, involves such an extreme downward action. The idea that this groove is evidence of the frequent use of water transport is given support when we look at the incidence of it in various parts of the country. The Chatham Islanders, the Moriori, lack such grooves, or show them only to a slight degree. The Chathams lie isolated in the Roaring Forties surrounded by a very rough ocean, and lack any substantial trees with which to make canoes. One would not expect the Moriori to be great seafarers. Their voyaging seems to have been limited to journeys between the two main islands, and occasional trips to the albatross rocks of the Forty-Fours. For these journeys they possessed only small, fragile canoes of planks sewn together. Most of their food came from the seashore, the lake, the lagoon and the bush, and nowhere was a substantial amount of paddling required.

By contrast, the inhabitants of the Coromandel Peninsula and its off-lying islands, and the Waitemata, show conspicuous rib grooves on the clavicles, more pronounced on one side, and more often right than left. Here, a physical feature may offer information on social things. The earlier material from the thirteenth and fourteenth century, shows these rib grooves in both male and female. Material from the latter prehistoric shows them only in males. It is known that in this later period fishing and the use of canoes for warfare were essentially male activities. A possible inference is that in the earlier days of settlement such division of activities did not exist, particularly with regard to fishing.

Some further evidence that this interpretation of clavicular grooves as evidence of extensive use of canoes is found when we come to look at the spine. The upper part of the spine, made up of the seven neck vertebrae, shows more frequent and more advanced arthritis in individuals with prominent rib grooves on their clavicles (*Fig. 7.5*). Paddling a canoe (with a single, not double, paddle) throws a considerable strain on the neck and causes very real discomfort in those not accustomed to it, and it seems reasonable to relate all these skeletal findings to the one cause. This inverse relationship between neck and low back degeneration reasonably suggests that those groups who were not able to use canoe transport regularly in their day-to-day activities were obliged to carry heavy loads on their backs.

The leg, like the arm, shows prominent ridges for the attachment of muscles and tendons, and impressions on the neck of the femur of the ligaments of the hip joint where they were pressed firmly against the bone in individuals who vigorously ran up and down and across the land. The tilt of the plateau of the tibia (*Fig. 3.8*) where it enters the knee joint, has been previously described, and may be a consequence of habitual squatting. There is other evidence of the frequent assumption of this position — the lower

Fig. 7.6: *Transverse grooves in the enamel of the teeth may be evidence of stress – illness or an inadequate diet.*

end of the tibia and the uppermost of the foot bones show distinct impressions or facets where these two bones are pressed together as the leg bends forward on the foot. These 'squatting' facets are, of course, in no way distinctive of these Polynesians, but are found in all groups that have this habit of resting.

After the bones, there are the ever-valuable teeth to be considered. As we have seen, they may give clues as to origins and relationships. In response to stress, inadequate diet or illness, they may show deficiencies in their enamel, which appear as transverse lines on the teeth (*Fig. 7.6*). They are also valuable in ageing, and they offer information about the diet of times past, for they are a mirror or a template of what has passed between them in life.

The diet of the tropical Polynesia from which first New Zealanders emanated is fairly soft — bread-fruit, yams, coconut, seafish, and so on — and the teeth are not much worn, albeit rather more worn than those of most modern people eating a Western diet. Such a soft diet and lack of wear bring their own problems, as most of us well know. There may be a significant incidence of dental caries, and also disease of the gums and the underlying bone. The latter state is more usual in the prehistoric tropical record, and we shall place such gum and bone affections under the general title of periodontal disease. This may, but usually does not, co-exist with dental caries. Advanced periodontal disease may lead to extreme erosion of the bones supporting the teeth with subsequent tooth loss, and during the process a bad breath.

When the pattern of tooth wear in prehistoric New Zealand is studied, an intriguing picture emerges. The earlier inhabitants — before about AD 1500 — show a pattern of wear fairly similar, though perhaps slightly more severe with equivalent age, to the inhabitants of the islands of Eastern Polynesia. At the age of twenty years the enamel on the occlusal (chewing and contact) surface of the first molar, which has now been subjected to some fourteen years of wear, is only just worn through in two or three places to expose the dentine beneath. The front teeth, particularly the incisors, show rather more advanced wear, with larger patches of dentine. (Dentine is still a very hard substance, not much behind enamel in this respect, and there is plenty of strength left in the tooth.) Over the next twenty years of life, wear proceeds slowly but inexorably, with the emphasis continuing to be rather more on the front teeth than the back teeth.

This slow rate of tooth wear suggests a rather soft diet, and one that is unlikely to keep the gums massaged and healthy. Like their Pacific forebears, these early New Zealanders show a high incidence of erosion of the bone supporting the teeth, evidence of periodontal disease, and the associated deposition on the necks of the teeth of significant amounts of a calcium compound called calculus (*Fig. 7.7*). By the time some reached their thirties, this damage to the supporting bone was so severe that the roots of some teeth became loose, and the teeth were gradually lost. (The modern Polynesian also seems to have a particular susceptibility to periodontal disease.) Caries also occurred, but not commonly.

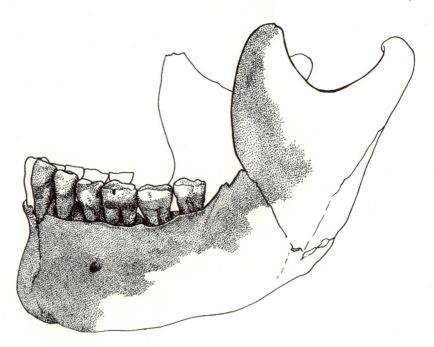

Fig. 7.7: *This man from Wairau Bar shows erosion of the bone supporting the teeth, evidence of periodontal disease.*

As we stressed when talking earlier about body form, it is rash to generalize. Before, this was because generalizations and averages might obscure significant regional differences, and hints of different origins and migrations. Here, with the teeth, it is necessary to be cautious because there is no doubt that food sources and diet varied considerably between different parts of the country, at the same period. Nevertheless, a generalization appears at present to be valid. From sites as separated as the Coromandel Peninsula, Castlepoint, Wairau Bar and coastal Otago, the pre-AD 1500 material shows this picture of slight tooth wear, and a related moderate incidence of periodontal disease. After about AD 1500 — this date is only suggested as an approximate watershed, and the dangers of generalization are all around — there is remarkable change in the pattern of tooth wear. This now occurs rapidly, with the enamel of the occlusal surface of the first molar sometimes being worn away completely to expose the dentine before the second molar has erupted, at about twelve years. *Fig. 7.8* shows lower molars of an eighteen-year-old woman from the Kaikoura Coast who lived about AD 1700 and whose first molar is worn to the roots. Such early and extreme wear is widespread throughout the country in the later prehistoric period. There seem to be no recent prehistoric — say post AD 1600 — individuals showing the lesser pattern of wear of the earlier prehistoric period.

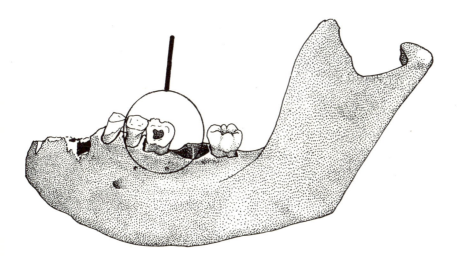

Fig. 7.8: *This 18-year-old woman from the Kaikoura coast in the later prehistoric, has worn away both enamel and dentine from her first molar, which will be lost in a matter of weeks.*

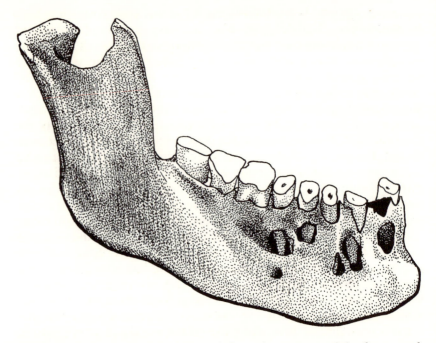

Fig. 7.9: *A rough diet has exposed the pulp cavities of the front teeth, and abcess formation around the roots has followed, with erosion of the bone. Usually this occurs in the back (molar) teeth first.*

With the change in wear comes a change in the related pathology, the related disease processes. After the enamel is worn away from the occlusal surface of the teeth, the hard dentine is well able to cope with the chewing forces for a time. But gradually the crown of the tooth is worn away and the chewing surface approaches closer and closer to the sensitive and all important pulp cavity, containing the nerves and blood vessels. As a reaction to the increasing pressure on this sensitive area, more dentine (secondary dentine) is produced within the tooth, filling in the most superficial part of the pulp cavity and preventing its exposure. Eventually even this is insufficient, and the pulp cavity is exposed on the occlusal surface. Infection now races through to the tips of the roots of the tooth, and an abcess forms around the root, in the supporting bone (*Figs. 7.9* and *7.10*). Quickly — in a matter of weeks probably — the tooth is lost.

This pattern of extreme wear, exposure of the pulp cavity, abcess formation around the roots, and tooth loss, occurs with monotonous regularity in the individuals from the later prehistoric period. There is a difference also in the site of maximum

122

wear in the dental arch. Wear on the front teeth is not marked, and maximum wear occurs on the first molar, which is nearly always the first tooth to be lost. Periodontal disease, calculus formation, and dental caries, are almost non-existent in the populations of the later period.

Another difference in the pattern of wear between the two periods is found particularly, if not exclusively, on the first molars, both upper and lower. It is very common to find in the later prehistoric period that these become worn not only on their occlusal surfaces, but also on their outer surfaces. The worn areas are continuous, passing smoothly from the occlusal to the outer surface, and the dentine of the entire area is highly polished. Gradually the whole tooth slips sideways, apparently under the pressure being exerted on it, and the roots of the teeth start to protrude through the bone. Eventually the tooth may come to lie completely exposed, and sideways, on the bone (*Fig. 7.11*). The pulp cavity is inevitably exposed by this stage and the usual sequence of infection, abcess formation and tooth loss follows. This form of wear is called, picturesquely if inaccurately, a 'fern-root plane', and we shall say a little more about it later.

This later pattern of more severe tooth wear certainly leads to earlier loss of teeth. It is common to find first molars missing by the age of twenty-five and those surviving to forty years in the later prehistoric period are near-edentulous, any remaining teeth being usually the non-functioning third molars (because they do not meet effectively with their partners) and the incisors. Bet-

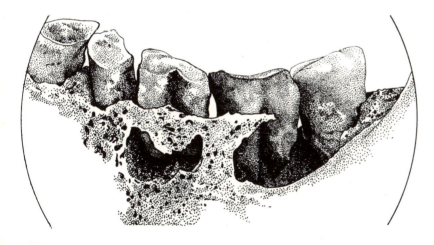

Fig. 7.10: *Another example of erosion, this time around the molar teeth, as a result of the wear from a rough diet.*

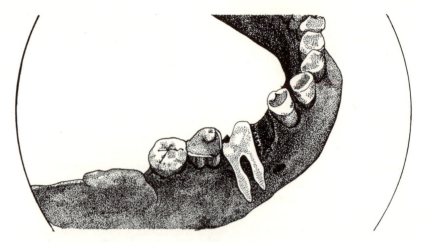

Fig. 7.11: *The 'fern-root plane' where the first molar has dislocated sideways out of the bone.*

ween, the teeth and their supporting bone have disappeared, giving a characteristic appearance, shown in *Fig. 7.12*.

Change of diet must be the basis of this change in the pattern of tooth wear, and a study of the factors involved here starts to a lead beyond mere biological anthropology. Three factors at least can be considered to have led to changes in the diet of these prehistoric New Zealanders. The disappearance of some common components of the earlier diet; climatic change — which bears on the first factor; and increasing population.

The earlier pattern of wear suggests a soft diet, and with the emphasis on the front teeth, a diet with a considerable amount of meat, where the tearing and cutting function of the incisors is required. It is to be noted that when the back teeth are worn to the dentine their enamel rims form effective cutting edges and they are not necessarily the pure grinding implements they are sometimes assumed to be. Nevertheless, in attacking a large piece of meat it is the front teeth on which the demands are made.

The answers to this problem of apparent dietary change are probably going to come, in the main, from the meticulous analysis archaeologists make of middens — the rubbish-heaps of prehistoric communities. From these assorted piles of shell and bone an astonishing amount of information about the activities and diet of these communities can be built up. To (dangerously) generalize, it does seem that with the passage of centuries the contents of middens become more monotonous, less varied, until in the later prehistoric they are limited in any coastal area to two or three varieties of shell-fish, a similar range of fish and two or three birds. In earlier centuries the animal remains are more varied, and there is a greater representation of larger animals, such as seals, and now-extinct birds, including the moa.

While the earlier people have been called moa-hunters it has been said that there is no evidence that the moa formed a substantial component of the diet for any group. However, while moa bones may seldom form a substantial component of middens, no hunter with a thought for his back would unnecessarily carry heavy bones encased in meat all the way to his camp — it is far more likely that the meat would be boned at the site of kill, and that the evidence of this component of the diet might be minimal at the site of habitation (though the larger bones were often turned into tools). A large animal offers a much better return in food for energy expended than do smaller animals for an equivalent portion. Again, it has been suggested that a number of New Zealand's bird species were effete, and naturally dying out over the past few centuries, and that man has had not very much to do with their extinction, or near-extinction. This seems a bit far fetched, and remarkably coincidental with the impact of man. For some early groups of New Zealanders the larger birds, and

Fig. 7.12: *A common end-result of the tooth wear caused by the rough diet of the later prehistoric period; only the third molars and a few front teeth remain.*

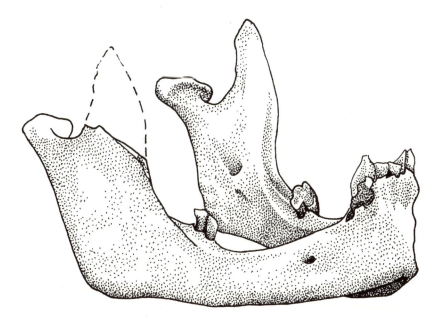

particularly the moa, may have formed a substantial and easily obtained component of the diet. As it was pursued to extinction, human life may have quite suddenly in some regions become a much more difficult thing to sustain. There is also evidence that by changing the environment, more particularly in the South Island, by burning off the forest and thereupon creating more grassland, the early New Zealanders hastened the extinction of the larger moas by removing their food resources.

We have mentioned the evidence, particularly botanical, from the growth rings of trees and of long-living lichens in sub-alpine areas, that there has been considerable climatic change in New Zealand in the past one thousand years. This is not surprising when we consider the well documented changes in climate in the northern hemisphere, such as the 'Little Ice Age' between about 1650 and 1850, when in Britain the Thames and sometimes parts of the sea froze. Since that time there has been a progressive warming in Britain, with an increase in average temperature of 1° centigrade in the past thirty years. This apparently insignificant change adds two weeks to each end of the growing season in Europe — an extra month of growing and cropping time. The implications for food production, particularly in previously marginal areas, are enormous. A similar rise has been recorded in parts of coastal Otago in little more than a century, in European times.

If the climate was warmer, then the first settlers, perhaps around AD 800, would have found a congenial soil for their tropical plants — the kumara, taro and yam. It is suggested that in this earlier period the kumara in particular was a major component of the diet — soft, and easy on the teeth. As the cold began to bite, kumara cultivation, always marginal in the south, retreated northward and northward, and elaborate precautions such as the construction of special storage pits were necessary to keep them, and preserve the source of the next season's crop.

Here, then, are two possible reasons for the change from soft to hard diet with the centuries — the extinction of easily obtained large sources of meat, and the harsher climate that rendered the kumara less available for much of the country.

What replaced these components of the diet? For protein, it seems to have partly been a descent into a scrabbling for shellfish of various species, rather arduous of preparation and collection, and gritty — an effective grinding paste for the teeth. Sea mammals figure occasionally, fish of course, dog, and later middens commonly throw up scraps of human bone. Sometimes the evidence for cannibalism is clear, as in *Fig. 7.13* of a young woman from the eastern Coromandel who was hit on the head a couple of centuries ago, decapitated, and the remains taken elsewhere. (Some of the early European writers have vivid accounts of the mode of preparation of bodies for such feasts, which involved a cutting off of hands and feet and then a remarkable filleting out out of the backbone, ribs, and long bones of the limbs, until the corpse was neatly rolled up, rather like a beef olive.) But human flesh is unlikely to have been more than an occasional luxury.

The vegetable component that to some extent supplanted kumara was fern root. Good sources of fern root were prized, and the bush was fired to make new clearings for the plant to invade. Naturally, fern root is fibrous, tough, demands considerable chewing, and would also be quite effective at wearing down the teeth. A 'flour' could be prepared from it by pounding with stone, but such a 'flour' is unlikely, considering the time involved, to have been a substantial component of diet.

Fig. 7.13: *This young woman was killed by a blow to the back of the head a couple of centuries ago.*

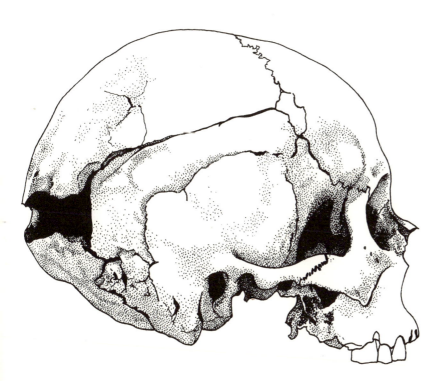

It seems likely also that increasing population in the north, perhaps accentuated then as now by the climate, led to greater demands on the available food resources, and a need to use those previously ignored. At the time of first European contact with the Waitemata the population seems to have been very dense indeed, though it was soon to be reduced by tribal wars.

Whatever the reasons archaeologists may finally ascertain for this change in diet over the centuries — the evidence for it etched in the teeth — the factors and components mentioned here are likely to prove significant, though the situation will be more subtle, more involved, and more regional than these generalizations suggest.

Before leaving the teeth we must again look at that curious feature of the later prehistoric, the fern-root plane. The name implies that it is a consequence of eating fern-root, which is reasonable enough as far as it goes — fern-root was certainly a

Fig. 7.14: *The natural curve formed by the teeth meeting tends to be particularly marked in the presence of the rocker jaw.*

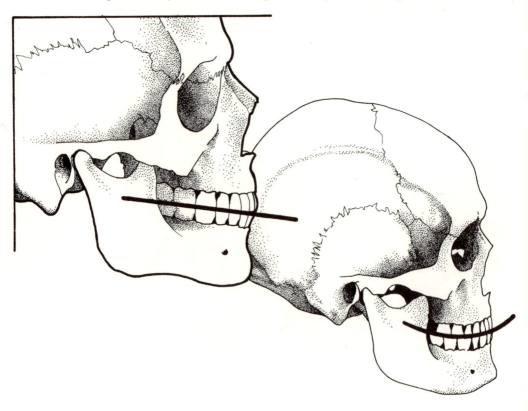

considerable component of the later diet. It has been suggested that it arose from the habit of chewing dried sticks of root, particularly on long journeys, these being placed into the side of the mouth between the first molars. This picture is a bit too simple. The habit would have had to be indulged in very regularly for such wear to predominate in the dentition, and it is noticeable that the wear is usually symmetrical — that is, the same on right and left sides. This implies that the individual carefully judged when he'd done enough chewing on one side, and switched to the other side to bring that down a bit. It seems more probable that this particular feature is a consequence of a generally fibrous and gritty diet. The Polynesian dental arch usually shows a particularly marked natural curve (the curve of Spee) when viewed from the side, with the bottom of the curve lying between the first molars, and this curve may well be related to the form of the rocker jaw (*Fig. 7.14*). This, and the fact that the mechanics of the mandible ensure maximal chewing forces between the first molars, is sufficient to suggest that it is the overall roughness of the diet that matters, not any specific, customary component prepared in a particular way. The feature has been noted in other races, such as the Australian Aborigine, who lack sticks of fern root. But the term is picturesque, widely known by anthropologists, and worth retaining.

Table 7.1

Thickness of the cortex of the second metacarpal (hand bone) on X-ray

Group	Occupation	Thickness in mm
American	mainly sedentary	5·9
Finnish	farmers	5·7
Norwegian	lumberjacks	5·6
Finnish	sedentary	5·2
N.Z. Polynesian	prehistoric, physically active	5·2

8. Disease

There is a fascination in looking at the evidence of disease from the past, yet it is a study that may be curiously irrelevant to the overall picture of the life of a prehistoric population. Bone is not always affected by disease in the body — we can seldom say precisely the cause of death in the past — and when it is involved there are only three possible responses; erosion, proliferation, or altered structure. For this reason it is often extremely difficult to assign a firm cause to an observed change — one ends with a list of possibilities, sometimes tantalising, sometimes as confusing as enlightening.

Preservation of soft tissues, as in mummies, can add greatly to the story. It is significant, for example, to the rule and accomplishments of Dynastic Egypt to know that even then the minute, waterborne, snail-dependent parasite, Bilharzia, was present in the population. This debilitating gut and liver parasite would have been a good ally of the Pharaohs. It is hard to raise a revolution when one can scarcely raise a foot. Again, from mummified remains in Peru it has been now proved that tuberculosis existed in the New World before the time of Columbus, with various interesting implications.

Bone is harder material to wring answers from. And there are other problems in looking at the diseases of the first New Zealanders. When considering their physique we were able to call on the observations and recordings of early Europeans. When it comes to illness we can place no such reliance on their observations, for the simple reason that European medicine was itself in a very primitive state at that time. While there are a few descriptions of identifiable disease, the lack of understanding of the basis of pathology, of the tissue reactions and the existence of bacteria, leads to an opaque quality in the medical writings of the past. So often one can only guess at the disease the writer is describing.

In short, though there may be a fascination in looking at evidence of disease from the past, the interpretation of this evidence is difficult and its contribution to the overall picture of prehistoric life may be limited.

Curiously, the first group of diseases on which we can make firm comment leave no mark on bone — unless it be a non-specific 'line of arrested growth'. The first New Zealanders did not suffer from our common 'childhood' infectious diseases such as measles, German measles (rubella), scarlet fever, mumps and chicken pox, nor the more serious ones such as smallpox. These diseases require a definite minimum size of population in which to survive and maintain themselves, and this pool may be as low as six thousand for measles or as high as fifty thousand for rubella. Nothing like these required numbers would have existed for the early settlers in New Zealand, nor indeed for millennia across the Pacific. These people, pushing on to island after island, generation after generation, effectively strained out most infections they might have started with. The same situation probably has applied to most of mankind for most of our time on the planet — most groups effectively lived in islands of existence scattered across continents, with insufficient contact to maintain these diseases. They have probably evolved quite recently — say in the past five thousand years — in the history of mankind. The populations in the regions in which they developed acquired resistance, at least after a time, partly by antibodies in the blood and partly perhaps by selection, so that the diseases usually became rather minor illnesses. But when virgin populations unacquainted with the virus or bacteria were suddenly exposed the results were tragic. Measles devastated many Pacific Islands. An Hawaiian king and his consort died of measles while visiting London in 1824, and their attending physicians, including Sir Henry Halford, President of the Royal College of Physicians, found it hard to believe that a disease "which even a delicate London girl might bear could be so destructive to the robust denizens of the Pacific." In 1848 every child born in Hawaii is said to have died of measles, whooping cough or influenza. Even allowing for exaggeration, the mortality must have been great. As recently as 1874, twenty thousand Fijians died of measles introduced from Australia. In New Zealand, observers in the later part of the nineteenth century spoke of whole villages deserted, annihilated by disease such as typhoid. And there is no evidence that the Pacific Islanders passed back to the invaders anything malign, except the odd knock on the head. Their populations were simply too small to maintain or originate such diseases.

If there is little doubt that acute infectious diseases were absent from New Zealand and the Pacific in prehistory, the more chronic infections offer more scope for debate. (Note that 'acute' means of sudden onset and short duration and has no reference to severity. 'Chronic' means of longer onset and duration.) Such diseases include tuberculosis, leprosy, yaws and syphilis.

Tuberculosis in man has a long history. There is evidence of it from Egypt as far back as 3000 BC and possibly earlier. There has been much debate as to whether it occurred in the New World before the time of Columbus, and until recently the informed opinion has been that it did not. Certainly in many parts of America, even in recent times, the impact of tuberculosis on the native populations has been devastating, suggesting a lack of previous contact. Recently the small rod-shaped tubercle bacillus has been identified in Peruvian mummies dating to the pre-Columbian era. In the Pacific there does not yet seem to be convincing evidence of its existence in prehistory. In populations with little resistance to the disease the changes are principally confined to the lungs and the disease is frequently fatal. In populations with more resistance bony changes start to appear, and these tend to form and persist over a longer period, not necessarily leading to the death of the individual. A common bony change is in the spine, where the joint (disc) between two vertebrae becomes softened and disintegrates, with gradual involvement of the adjacent bones. These collapse towards one another causing an angulation of the spine. This form, this imprint, of the disease is classical, and it is difficult to accept isolated diagnoses of tuberculosis from the remains of early populations when these spinal changes have not been noted. If this change is accepted as the bony hallmark of tuberculosis, then there is not yet evidence of it in New Zealand or other parts of Polynesia in prehistory. Certainly its ravages on a susceptible population was a major cause of the decline of the Maori to about forty thousand people at the turn of this century.

Leprosy, unlike tuberculosis, to which its bacillus is related, has a place in tradition. Buck relates how it was brought to New Zealand in two canoes, *Moekakara* and *Te Wakatuwhenua,* and the general belief seems to be that it occurred both in New Zealand and through the Pacific in prehistory. Robert Louis Stevenson even wrote a Pacific story around the theme of leprosy — *The Bottle Imp*. From the last century are a number of reports purported to be accurate descriptions of leprosy in New Zealand. I must confess I am not yet convinced as to the existence of leprosy as we now understand it in prehistoric New Zealand. Certainly there do not seem to be bony examples of the disease — leprosy attacks the bones of the face, and the extremities, fingers and toes, in a distinctive, eroding manner. However, this absence of evidence could be explained by the likely fate of the sufferer of such a disfiguring and lingering disease. He would be cast out of the community to fend for himself beyond reach of others — not for any reason of contagion or knowledge of spread of disease, but because traditional interpretation of the illness would ascribe it to infringement of some particularly virulent tapu. But a point in support of its existence in the Pacific in prehistory is some

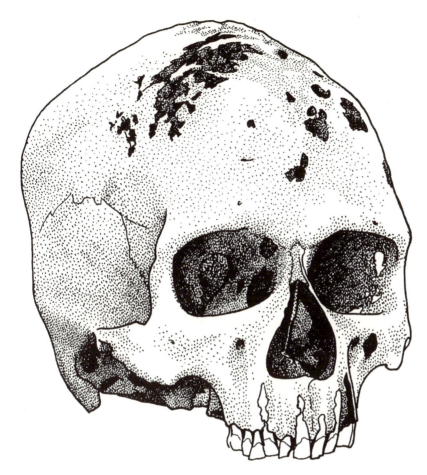

Fig. 8.1: *This example of yaws deeply eroding the vault of the skull comes from the Western Pacific.*

evidence in written accounts of its occurrence in China early in the first millennium BC. The suggestion is that the disease originated in Asia and only reached Europe early in the Christian era. Perhaps the first venturers into the Pacific, millennia ago, carried it with them, a disease capable of survival in such groups, small in number yet in close contact for long periods in cramped canoes. And we do now have a solitary finger bone from the Lau Islands in Fiji, dated to about 500 BC, which shows erosion and X-ray change consistent with leprosy — a little digit of support for a body of supposition.

Yaws and syphilis are two related diseases caused by spiral or corkscrew-shaped bacteria. Yaws is a disease of skin and bone, extremely common in the tropical Pacific in prehistory and until quite recently. It is not a venereal disease but is spread by contact to broken skin surfaces. It leads to extensive ulceration of the skin, which becomes secondarily infected with other bacteria. The unfortunate sufferer in times past had little chance of achieving a cure. The bone beneath the skin lesions becomes gradually involved, and two common sites for this to happen are the shins, when the front of the tibia become eroded, and the forehead, when the vault of the skull is eroded — sometimes very deeply with complete penetration of the bone (*Fig. 8.1*). From the tropical Pacific — Polynesia, Melanesia and Micronesia — there is such bony evidence, eroded skulls and misshapen limb bones, but on the long journey south to New Zealand it was lost, probably because the cooler climate is inimical to it. We have no bony evidence of yaws from New Zealand prehistory.

The origin of the related syphilis is one of the great puzzles of historical medicine. Its apparently abrupt appearance and violence in the last years of the fifteenth century in Europe — the 'great pox' as opposed to the 'small pox' — led to the general belief that it was brought back from the Americas by Columbus' expedition. However, the evidence for syphilis in pre-Columbian America is not impressive. The bony changes are really identical with yaws, and there are few enough of them from early America. (The assumption that yaws, not syphilis, was the disease in the Pacific rests on what was later determined to be prevalent.) While it is possible that the organism was brought from America and attained a new virulence in a susceptible population — an unusual turn of events for the European — it is as likely that it came out of Asia, or even had existed previously in Europe and perhaps attained this new virulence through mutation. One view of the relationship between yaws and syphilis is that yaws developed first, in warm, moist climates, on warm, moist skin surfaces. When groups of mankind moved to cooler climates the organism was able only to survive on the warm, moist inner body surfaces, and venereal transmission became a reliable vehicle for it. Anyway, we have no evidence of the existence of syphilis in New Zealand in prehistory. The Europeans nurtured it, lovingly, and carried it away round the world with them again. While it takes us a little out of our prehistoric context, it is interesting to note that we cannot be sure of the impact of syphilis on the New Zealanders. Early missionary accounts from the Bay of Islands suggest that venereal disease was rife outside their folds. Yet at least one medical authority of the latter part of the century maintained that while this may have been true for gonorrhoea —

with its implications for sub-fertility or sterility and decline of a race — it just was not true for syphilis. Dr Newman's comments, made in 1881, are worth quoting in full, and are supported by the complete lack of skeletal evidence for syphilis in the early part of the last century:

> Many observers not trained in medicine talk about the frightful effects of that 'awful scourge' syphilis, and say that the Maori population is saturated with it, and that its fearful effects are seen in the sterility of the race and the astonishing mortality existing among the children. To this disease I have paid special attention and made special enquiries from doctors — the only class of men whose opinion is worth taking — and they confirm me in the belief that, though the Maoris are affected by it, yet its results are rarely severe. My own feeling (remembering the frightful scourge it proved on its introduction to various parts of Europe) is one of astonishment at the smallness of the evil. Several doctors who practice largely among the Maoris assure me that they never saw true syphilis in a Maori. My own experience is that amongst the large number of Maoris I have seen I have not been able to detect any evils from this cause, yet I am quite sure that in any like number of low-living whites the evidences would be abundant. I have never seen Maori children with any marks of syphilis. Though I have searched everywhere and have tried to seek confirmatory evidence of the reports of the frightful ravages of syphilis, I am forced to the conclusion that they are unfounded, and that syphilis has been a very unimportant one among the many factors leading to the decrease of the Maoris.

From small parasites like bacteria to larger parasites like worms. To this day many Pacific populations carry heavy infestations of intestinal worms, particularly roundworm and hookworm. The former, in small doses, is not a particularly offensive parasite, and need not cause its host significant harm. (It is a poor parasite that kills its host.) In larger infestations it can cause a failure to thrive, or even blockage of the intestine. All in all, if not an attractive thing it is an organism not particularly worrying to the health of the community. Hookworm is more serious. The mature worm clings to the wall of the intestine and sucks blood from the host. This may readily lead to anaemia, and general ill-health and a susceptibility to infections, and can be a significant factor in the failure of a group to succeed in their environment. For these reasons it would be interesting to know

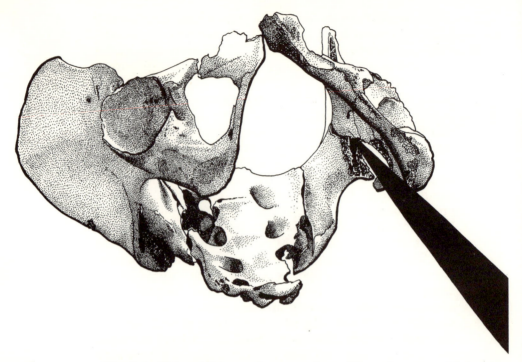

Fig. 8.2: *This middle-aged woman from fifteenth-century Wairarapa died as a result of a spear thrust to the pelvis.*

the load of intestinal parasites carried by man to New Zealand from the tropical Pacific. On first consideration it might seem blatantly impossible to ever determine such facts, but this is not so.

The microscopic eggs of these intestinal parasites pass out in the faeces encased in extremely hard shells designed to resist desiccation. This they do very successfully. They also resist disintegration with time. In suitable situations archaeologists may excavate dried, still recognizable human faeces, which go by the name of coprolites. When these specimens are rehydrated by suitable techniques and examined under the microscope the eggs of these parasitic intestinal worms may be recognizable by those experienced in such diagnosis. In this way hookworm is known to have existed amongst various North and South American prehistoric populations. There is evidence that roundworm is European in origin, carried by them to the New World, and perhaps the Pacific. In New Zealand there has been little work yet done on coprolites, but when the growing assemblage of them comes to be examined, something of the existence of these parasites in

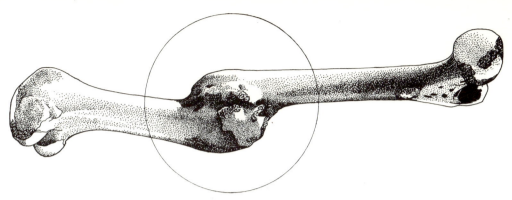

Fig. 8.3: *This femur has broken in the middle of the shaft. Despite some overlap and shortening, the healing was sound and this person could have continued to live an active life, though he would have walked with a limp.*

prehistoric New Zealand may be learned. Of course it is quite possible, even likely, that the parasites were brought to New Zealand and gradually died out — there is nothing in early European medical reports to suggest that worms were a significant health problem. The New Zealand climate was probably too cool for the hookworm larvae to survive, as they must, for periods on vegetation and the ground adjacent to latrines. Both species also are favoured by higher densities of population, more likely to be achieved on small islands or in sophisticated agricultural communities. It is likely that the first New Zealanders were too few and perhaps too mobile for these parasites to survive.

Less esoteric, more obvious in the health record of the past should be injuries to the skeleton — fractures and dislocations. But to those accustomed to the carnage of the machine age these are rather uncommon. We know of isolated examples of fractures of just about every bone — forearm bones, ribs, finger bones, collar bones and jaw bones and the vault of the skull. We are talking particularly of fractures that show evidence of healing — by union of the ends and rounded edges — indicating that the sufferer survived a long period after the incident: though sometimes, as in the case of the girl from seventeenth century Coromandel (*Fig. 7.13*) the evidence for deliberate assault, and immediate death, is convincing. And from thirteenth century Wairarapa comes unusually clear evidence of death by violence — a middle-aged woman has had a spear thrust forcibly into her pelvis which would have led to death within a few days, if not immediately (*Fig. 8.2*) But the healed fractures we observe have generally resulted in an adequate, functioning limb, shortened an inch or so in the case of a major bone like the femur (*Fig. 8.3*), but

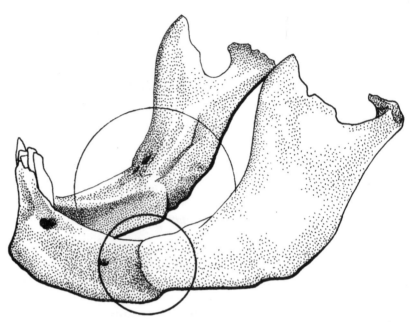

Fig. 8.4: *This mandible was broken in two places. Healing has been good, but most of the teeth have been lost.*

good enough for vigorous living. A fractured jaw (*Fig. 8.4*), however, often led to the loss of some teeth and this could lead to a steady decline in health in the longer term, considering the harshness of the diet.

Dislocations hardly appear — probably most were adequately treated, returned to position by rough and painful manipulation. We know an example of dislocation of the hip that was not put back in place, and the individual lived on for years and painful years, with the deformed head of the femur carving out for itself a new, rough socket on the side of the hip (*Fig. 8.5*). It is possible that this is an example of the dislocation of the hip that may exist at birth, and the boy grew up with it.

In general then, fractures and dislocations, deliberate or accidental injury to the skeleton, are uncommon, and interestingly there is scarcely an example of the common fracture of some prehistoric communities, the 'parrying fracture', where the bones of the (usually left) forearm have been broken when attempting to fend off a forceful blow. We don't have enough data to be able to say that evidence of deliberate injury increases with time, into the later prehistoric, as pressure on land and food resources grew, and the evidence of the fortifications is that warfare became endemic.

Fig. 8.5: *This man lived until his early thirties with a long-standing dislocation of his left hip. The distorted upper end of the femur (thigh bone) has partly formed a new socket for itself.*

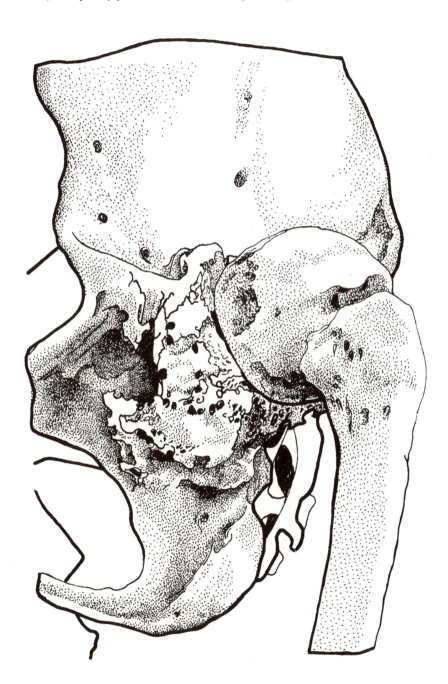

If acute injury is uncommon, then a slower deformation of the skeleton in the shape of various forms of arthritis is widespread, is almost the normal pattern in anyone over the age of twenty-five years. The situation is akin to that observed with the teeth which were considered under *Health* but could equally, in the later stages of their wear, be considered under *Disease* — the borderland is undefined. Extreme physical activity can wear out any bony component of the body. In the bony framework, as we have seen, it is particularly the spine that gives way, for this has been a weak point ever since we got up on two legs. These blocks of spongy bone piled one on top of the other and bearing all the weight of the upper body as well as any loads carried, were simply not designed for the job. In these prehistoric New Zealanders the pattern seems to be, as suggested earlier, a degeneration of the lower spine in those who carried loads considerable distances and did not use canoes, such as at Wairau Bar, and a degeneration of the neck vertebrae in those who intensively used canoes. The degenerative changes, a lipping, flattening, and sometimes eventual fusion of the vertebrae, are often marked by twenty-five years, and few over thirty years of age show no such changes, particularly in the lower spine. Pain may have been considerable from some of these backs, though perhaps good muscles gave a natural splintage, a sort of built-in physiotherapy. In extreme cases such degeneration can lead to pressure on the spinal cord, and paralysis.

The joints of the limbs do not show such marked changes, being better designed biomechanically to resist extreme body strains. By the age of thirty most prehistoric New Zealanders are showing some minor arthritis in the major limb joints, a slight lipping at the very edges, but this may progress little over another decade. No consistent pattern of arthritis has been detected, to match certain patterns of activity such as using a spear for hunting and so on. But in the head, at the joint where the lower jaw meets the cranium, a flattening and slight arthritis is inevitable as the teeth wear down and the jaw moves forward slightly to maintain occlusion.

A disease which leaves an arthritic imprint on bone and yet whose basis is very different from the usual arthritis of extreme physical activity, is gout. This is a metabolic disease, in which the body is unable to cope normally with oxalate in the diet. Crystals of calcium oxalate become deposited in some of the soft tissues such as the lobe of the ear and the kidney — which may be serious in its effect on health — and in joints. Classically, the big toe is affected, the picture being of the puce-faced, somewhat over-

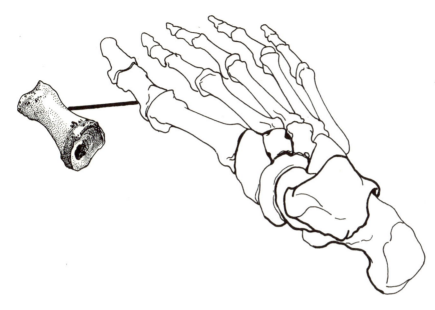

Fig. 8.6: *This erosion at the base of the big toe may be evidence of gout.*

weight English gentleman of yester-year sitting with his painful, bandaged foot up on a cushion, surrounded by bottles of port and other evidence of good living. Our present interest is in the fact that the modern Maori has a high incidence of gout, and knowledge of its existence or absence in prehistory is significant in determining the basis of this modern high incidence. There is evidence that the gout of the modern Maori is metabolically slightly different from the classical European form. There is evidence also of arthritic changes in the joints of big toes from prehistory that are compatible with the changes of gout (*Fig. 8.6*). Such evidence is at present equivocal and much more work needs to be done in unravelling the story. Conclusive proof would be identification of calcium oxalate crystals in prehistoric material, but as these are soluble in water such evidence is unlikely to be obtained.

In some disease processes the body forms hard structures other than bone, which may persist long after death. Particularly this applies to the stones — calcium compounds — that may form in the gall bladder, in the kidneys and in the urinary bladder. *Fig. 8.7* shows such a case, from the seventeenth century. This young woman was uncovered during excavations for a Government building — which was not built because of the findings on the site. She was in her early twenties, and meticulous excavation

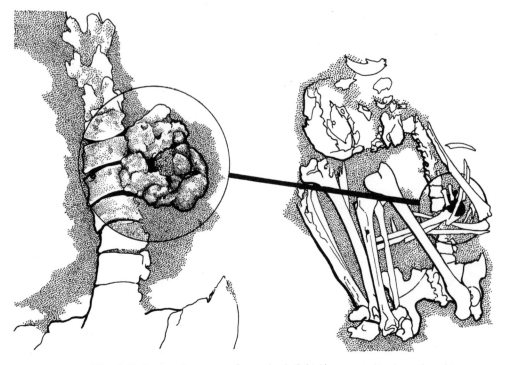

Fig. 8.7: *A massive stone from the left kidney was displayed in this young woman, buried in a crouch position.*

revealed a large hard mass on the left side of the spine, high up in the abdominal region. The appearance and position of this mass readily led to the diagnosis, confirmed by chemical analysis, that this was a massive stone in the left kidney. The chemical composition showed it to be of the type that tends to occur after repeated kidney infections, and examination of the pelvis showed that this woman had borne two or three children. Infections of bladder and kidney are a common complication of pregnancy and it seems reasonable to assume that repeated infections resulting from her pregnancies led to the development and growth of this very large stone. The specimen clearly shows the form of the distended cavity within the kidney. Its existence would have led to death as a result of severe kidney infection and spread in the blood stream. Kidney stones are not commonly recorded from prehistory and there seems no record of one as massive as this. More usually in the record of the past they have been formed in the bladder, where they may become very large indeed.

The various diseases of man tend to be associated with different phases of his life span, and the average life span of the population being studied must be considered before emphatic comments are made about the incidence of a disease in the group. If this is not done it is only a short jump to fallacious thoughts of "a remarkable immunity" to certain diseases, with the corollaries of former pristine environments, better diets, modern Western degeneration, refined foods and so on. This is evident when we look at two major causes of death in modern Western man, disease of the heart and arteries, and cancer.

Disease of heart and arteries is commonly regarded as a modern disease, consequent on a number of factors including a high fat diet, lack of exercise and smoking, and the assumption seems to be that its incidence in earlier societies was much less. Even some medical texts talk of "this modern scourge", and perhaps with a rather limited view of the world and history some medical authorities have proposed Draconian measures to drag modern society screaming into the healthy life.

There is no question that heart disease is less common amongst modern undeveloped societies than in those with a Western life-style, and we can say with confidence that it was also much lower in prehistoric times. One significant reason is clearly seen by looking at the graph of life spans of the people of Wairau Bar, or any other early population. These people would have been delighted to suffer from the modern scourge. As it was, few of them had the remotest chance of living to the dangerous age and to be struck down at the age of fifty by a heart attack would have been regarded by them as a venerable death. We have one or two hints from Polynesia that hardening of the arteries, the building up of calcium compounds in their walls, occurred at much the same rate as in modern societies. For example from the Chatham Islands we find extensive hardening of the major artery in the abdomen by the age of fifty, this diagnosis being proved microscopically, and evidence from Tonga of extensive hardening of the arteries of the limbs at an even earlier age. (It is relevant that certain components of the prehistoric New Zealand diet, such as smoked eel and crayfish, are high in cholesterol.) Rather, viewed in historical perspective, heart and artery disease is no modern scourge but an inevitable concomitant of ageing, of an older and older population. This is not denying local, racial and dietary factors entirely, which would be against good evidence, but they are small things against the inexorable process of ageing. The bones thin and the arteries thicken.

Cancer is often said to be a consequence of the deleterious

environment, in its widest sense, created by modern man, and there is sound evidence to support the view that the majority of cancers are related to the environment, to aspects of diet, habit, or pollution. It is thence assumed that early man would be free of such problems and his pure, unsullied environment is then emphasized. But if a graph showing the ages at which the maximum incidence of cancer occurs is combined with one showing the age at death of a typical prehistoric population, it is very clear that comparison between the incidence then and now is pointless. Cancer is essentially a disease of older people, from about sixty years onward, and prehistoric New Zealanders or any others just didn't live that long. Again, far from being a modern scourge, cancer appears as a concomitant of a physically healthy society. That it can be unpleasant is undeniable, and modern medicine justifiably spends considerable effort in improving methods of eliminating or alleviating it in the individual case. But a belief in the possibility of an overall cure for this spectrum of diseases is naive.

The other peak of cancer incidence besides the older age group is in children, and we might expect to find evidence in this group of cancer in prehistoric New Zealand. Yet is is still relatively uncommon in this group, and considering the inadequacy of the skeletal record and that cancer may not mark the bones, negative evidence is no evidence. But in the spine of an eleven-year-old girl from inland Canterbury who died about AD 1750, we find some suggestion of cancer. Several of the vertebrae from the thoracic (chest) region show smooth-walled erosion of their bodies, and at one point this has extended into the end of a rib (*Fig. 8.8*). The most likely diagnosis of this lesion is spread of cancer in the adrenal gland, a small hormone-producing gland that sits on top of the kidney. This cancer is peculiar to children and it must be admitted that she is getting a bit old for cancer of the adrenals. Nevertheless, it is still the likeliest diagnosis.

There seems no other convincing evidence of cancer in prehistoric New Zealanders. One other possibility worth mentioning is of a young woman aged about twenty years from Wairau Bar. The inner aspect of the bones of her cranium shows distinct erosions, up to two centimetres across, and it is just possible that these represent secondary spread of cancer from some other site (*Fig. 8.9*). But the most likely cause is a rather rare disease of unknown cause with the curious name of histiocytosis-X.

Diabetes is a disease of sugar metabolism, and modern Polynesians, Maori and other, have one of the highest incidences in the world — some 10 percent of most Polynesian groups living a

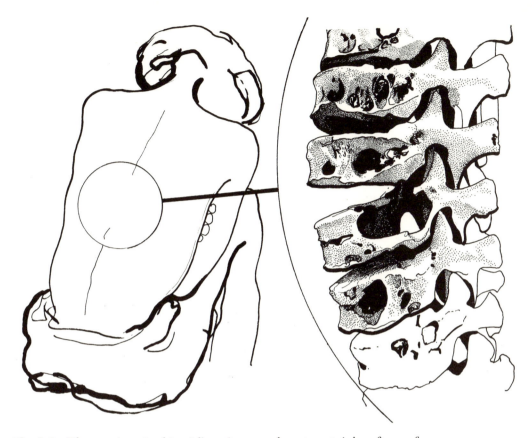

Fig. 8.8: *The erosions in this girl's spine are almost certainly a form of cancer.*

Westernized existence and studied from this point of view have been found to suffer from overt diabetes. Women show a higher incidence than men. There are similar findings in Australian Aboriginal groups on a Western diet. Some years ago an American geneticist J. V. Neel suggested the interesting concept of a 'thrifty genotype'. By this is meant a genetic influence on body metabolism that ensures maximal utilization of food intake. Such a metabolism will keep the blood sugar level adequate in the face of marginal food supply, and the survival advantage of this in groups leading a precarious existence in a difficult environment — be it on a barren atoll or the fringe of a desert — is obvious. But such an inheritance becomes a disadvantage with the change to a Westernized existence. Obesity and its attendant diabetes are probably modern evidence of a characteristic that assisted the ancestral Polynesians to survive.

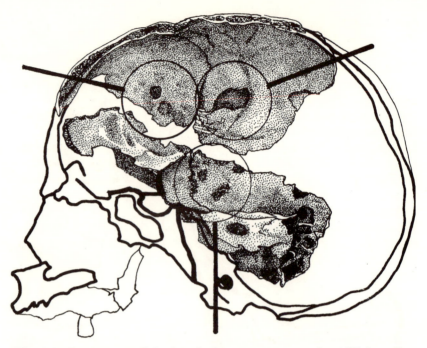

Fig. 8.9: *Fragments of the head of a young woman from Wairau Bar, showing unusual erosions in the bone.*

In prehistoric New Zealand, medical treatment in the modern sense was probably limited to the more obvious, external problems. Fractures were splinted, wounds cauterized with a hot stick, and counter-irritation in the form of scratches or cuts on the skin practised for the relief of deep-seated pain. Certain plant concoctions were used for minor ailments, such as an infusion of flax root for constipation, or the sap of the rata vine for wounds. Buck makes the point that only after European contact did the New Zealanders start to experiment more widely with native plants. The traditional belief was that illness was a consequence of the infringement of some tapu, and could only be alleviated by identification of the infringement by the *tohunga*, and some appropriate ritual or penance performed. As Buck comments, ''. . . the Maori *tohunga* made prior use of some, at least, of the methods of the modern psychoanalyst.'' This belief, that illness resulted from infringement of tapu, may well have led to the removal of people suffering from more mysterious, chronic and particularly disfiguring diseases such as leprosy from the immediate community, and explain early European comments on the absence of obviously sick people in the New Zealand villages.

9. Conclusions

What, in the end, is the picture these studies create?

The first New Zealanders had a distinctive physical form. Generally they were tall, robust people with proportionally shorter legs and longer arms than most Europeans. They had large, high-vaulted heads with a distinctive jaw form and a vertical face in profile. Much of their anatomy stands at one extreme of the range of growth and form of mankind, and this distinctiveness can be explained by the concepts of genetic drift and the 'founder effect'. Any small group plucked out of a population may not, in physical form, be typical of that population. Over millennia of Pacific voyaging there was ample opportunity for the founder effect to operate, yet the similarity of Polynesians over their territory suggests that this chance selection of physical form occurred at the very beginning of the settlement of what is now known as Polynesia. Archaeology is now starting to produce the skeletal evidence.

Beyond Polynesia the origins of the Polynesians are not yet clear. Chance selection from a variable group inhabiting the islands of Melanesia to the east of New Guinea in the second millennium BC, is a strong possibility. Too much should not be made of the assignment of Polynesians to a Mongoloid racial stock, and tortuous attempts to bring them out of island South-East Asia or even mainland Asia with pure genes, be it through Melanesia or Micronesia. The physical differences between Polynesians and Asians are considerable.

Within Polynesia, the western islands such as Tonga and Samoa were settled first, with later migration to the east, and thence to the distant, peripheral islands, Hawaii, Easter Island and New Zealand. The widely-known story of New Zealand's settlement by a Great Fleet in AD 1350 preceded by Toi, Kupe, and an earlier possibly Melanesian people, the 'Maruiwi', are European distortions and amalgamations of the genuine, regional traditions.

They were generally healthy. The same filter of ocean and islands that strained out genes also strained out diseases, and populations were not large enough to support the viruses and bacteria of more modern times and epidemics.

In discussing disease in New Zealand prehistory, our conclusions do seem to have been largely negative — no epidemics, few chronic diseases such as tuberculosis, no debilitating parasites, no heart disease, no cancer, few fractures, and a metabolism efficient in the face of minimal food supplies. Robust, strong adults. Yet average life span was no more than thirty years. The paradox requires comment.

To understand it, it is necessary to look back past a generation or so of the effective Western medicine to which we have become so accustomed to try and grasp what an illness or an injury has meant to an individual throughout most of mankind's time on this planet. Nowadays most illnesses and injuries may receive specific and fairly effective treatment. In the past there was scarcely an effective treatment for any disease, and treatment of injury was not especially helpful, particularly if infection could supervene. In other words the individual was almost entirely dependent on the inherent ability of his own bodily mechanisms for overcoming infection and repairing injury. Unassisted, these mechanisms cannot be regarded as particularly efficient. And all the various factors we have discussed add up. A man in his twenties, teeth partly rotted following wear from a rough diet, developing pneumonia in a damp *whare* in even a northern winter, was not a candidate for survival. Even less was the child, and still less the newborn. Pneumonia was probably a major killer, with the incidence in early childhood being particularly high. And despite the lack of epidemics there was no problem in finding the necessary bacteria — each of us carries bacteria fully capable of killing us if they get in the wrong place in sufficient number. It happens that most of the time they are confined in numbers and in situation.

A hard physical life left its stamp, and there are grounds for believing that man's physical framework, outside modern conditions, is designed for no more than forty years of wear. The importance of the teeth in survival terms has perhaps not been stressed enough — hard or soft diet, their natural life span, without modern assistance, seems around that forty years, and their disintegration and loss brought problems both of nutrition and infection. We should be less surprised at the natural history of disease in the past than appreciative of its unnatural course in the present.

In their adult lives, short by our standards, women bore on average three or four children. Fertility was suppressed by breast feeding, and sometimes by a marginal diet. Despite these limitations it is theoretically possible that New Zealand was settled once and once only by a very small group.

This story of a human population in the past is typical in many ways of the life of man in prehistory anywhere. Of course a major influence is the environment, and New Zealand was probably a favourable one despite its lack of large animals to supply meat. The climate is nowhere extreme and natural hazards are few. All in all, by the standards of global prehistory (and a great deal of history) physical life was generally good.

There is a vast amount to be done in further clarifying this story of the past. Clearer ideas on origins, settlement time and numbers will emerge. There needs to be a greater emphasis on physical life on a regional basis, for there is no doubt that resources and health varied from region to region and from generation to generation. The generalization that life was healthy, the people robust and the diet adequate, must be taken with caution, for more detailed studies are already starting to suggest that things were not quite as good as have appeared at our first glance. Further studies will also answer questions relevant to modern health such as the incidence of gout and of ear disease in the past. There is no doubt that our knowledge of this aspect of New Zealand's past will continue to grow — much has been done even in the time taken to write this book, and which cannot appear here.

I began by indicating that New Zealand was the last substantial area of land to be reached by man, yet that this relatively brief history of perhaps a thousand years was nonetheless fascinating. What has been related here is only one aspect, or version, of the rich past of this distinctive land, and these figures in the foreground should be looked at against the full sweep of land and migrations, culture and belief. In this spirit it is offered.

Bibliography

This selection is neither comprehensive nor particularly logical. A number of books or papers mostly directed at more general aspects of Oceanic or New Zealand prehistory are listed first: then some publications relevant to each chapter. Sometimes I have appended comments. The references given in recent publications will lead to relevant past material.

General

Bellwood, P., 1978. *Man's Conquest of the Pacific*. Collins, Auckland.

Buck, P. (Te Rangi Hiroa), 1950. *The Coming of the Maori* 2nd Ed. Whitcombe & Tombs, Wellington. (Inevitably dated in some matters, but still the best introduction to things Maori.)

Duff, R., 1956. *The Moa Hunter Period of Maori Culture* 2nd Ed. Govt. Printer, Wellington. (This major work of a generation ago is now very dated in some respects, particularly in its use of 'traditional' evidence.)

Davidson, J. M., 1978. Auckland Prehistory: A Review. *Records of the Auckland Institute and Museum*. Vol. 15, pp. 1-14.

Fox, A., 1976 *Prehistoric Maori Fortifications*. Longman Paul, Auckland.

Gluckman, L. K., 1976. *Tangiwai*. Whitcoulls, Wellington. (A collection of notes on aspects of Maori health in the nineteenth century — that is, post-European.)

Green, R. C., 1974. Adaption and Change in Maori Culture. In Kuschel, G. (Ed.). *Ecology and Biogeography in New Zealand*. W. Junk, The Hague.

Howells, W. W., 1973. *The Pacific Islanders*. Reed, Wellington. (A detailed study of the people of the Pacific by a leading physical anthropologist.)

Leach, B. F., and Leach, H. M. (Eds), 1979. Prehistoric Man in Palliser Bay. *National Museum of New Zealand, Bulletin No. 21*. (A major archaeological study of a New Zealand region, fully utilizing the various scientific disciplines relevant to archaeology.)

Snow, C. E., 1974. *Early Hawaiians*. The University Press of Kentucky, Lexington. (A readable account of a study of a large prehistoric Polynesian skeletal series.)

Two relevant New Zealand periodicals are the *New Zealand Archeological Association Newsletter* (Secretary, C/- Otago Museum, Great King Street, Dunedin), and the *Journal of the Polynesian Society* (P.O. Box 10323, The Terrace, Wellington).

The Archaeological Material
Detailed accounts of structure of bone are given in standard anatomical texts such as Gray or Cunningham. A clear, simplified account is in le Gros Clark, *Tissues of the Body* 6th Ed. Oxford.

Physique
Buck, P., 1922-23. Maori Somatology. *Journal of the Polynesian Society.* Vol. 31, pp. 37-44. (Gives the results of his examination of the members of the Maori Battalion returning from the First World War.)

Houghton, P., Leach, B. F., and Sutton, D. G., 1975. Estimation of Stature of Prehistoric Polynesians in New Zealand. *Journal of the Polynesian Society.* Vol. 84, pp. 325-336.

Schofield, G., 1959. Metric and Morphological Features of the Femur of the New Zealand Maori. *Journal of the Royal Anthropological Institute.* Vol. 89, pp. 89-106.

Thomson, A. S., 1859. *The Story of New Zealand* 2 vols. Murray, London. (As a medical officer Thomson made some valuable observations on Maori physique, health and disease. These volumes are available in a Capper Press reprint, P.O. Box 1388, Christchurch.)

Head Form
Dennison, K. J. In Press. Tooth Size and Sexual Dimorphism in Prehistoric New Zealand Polynesian Teeth. *Archeology and Physical Anthropology in Oceania.*

Houghton, P., 1978. Polynesian Mandibles. *Journal of Anatomy.* Vol. 127, pp. 251-260.

Marshall, D. S., and Snow, C. E., 1956. An Evaluation of Polynesian Craniology. *American Journal of Physical Anthropology.* Vol. 14, pp. 405-427.

Relations and Origins
Green, R. C., 1978. New Sites with Lapita Pottery and their Implications for an Understanding of the Settlement of the Western Pacific. *Working Paper No. 51,* Dept. of Anthropology, University of Auckland.

Lewis, D., 1972. *We, The Navigators.* Reed, Wellington.

Pawley, A., and Green, R. C., 1975. Dating the Dispersal of the Oceanic Languages. *Oceanic Linguistics.* Vol. 12, pp. 1-68.

Pietrusewsky, M., 1970. Osteological View of Indigenous Populations in Oceania. In Green, R. C., and Kelly, M. (Eds.), Studies in Oceanic Culture History Vol. 1. *Pacific Anthropological Records.* B. P. Bishop Museum.

Sharp, C. A., 1963. *Ancient Voyagers in Polynesia*. Paul, Auckland.

Simmons, D. R., *The Great New Zealand Myth.*. Reed, Wellington. (This critical analysis of the Great Fleet story is presented in terser form in his paper in the *New Zealand Journal of History* Vol. 3, pp. 14-31, 1969.)

Sorrenson, M. P. K., 1977. The Whence of the Maori: some nineteenth century exercises in scientific method. *Journal of the Polynesian Society*. Vol. 86, pp. 449-478. (A good account of the origins of some modern mythology.)

Turner, C. G., and Hanihara, K., 1977. Additional Features of the Ainu Dentition. V Peopling of the Pacific. *American Journal of Physical Anthropology* Vol. 46, pp. 13-24.

Life Span, Fertility and Population

Black, F. C., 1975. Infectious Diseases in Primitive Societies. *Science* Vol. 187, pp. 515-518.

Dennison, K. J. In Press. Citrate Estimation as a Means of Determining the Sex of Human Skeletal Material. *Archeology and Physical Anthropology in Oceania*.

Dumond, D. E., 1975. The Limitation of Human Populations: a Natural History. *Science* Vol. 187, pp. 713-721.

Houghton, P., 1975. The Bony Imprint of Pregnancy. *Bulletin of the New York Academy of Medicine* Vol. 51, pp. 655-661.

May, R. L., 1978. Human Reproduction. *Nature* Vol. 272, pp. 491-495.

Phillipps, M. A. L. *An Estimation of Fertility in Prehistoric New Zealanders*. Unpublished B.A. (Hons.) Thesis, University of Otago.

Health

Houghton, P., 1978. Dental Evidence for Dietary Variation in Prehistoric New Zealand. *Journal of the Polynesian Society*. Vol. 87, pp. 257-263.

Simpson, A. I. W. *Health and Disease in Prehistoric New Zealanders*. Unpublished B.Med.Sc. Thesis, University of Otago.

Taylor, R. M. S., 1963. Cause and Effect of Wear of Teeth. *Acta Anatomica*. Vol. 53, pp. 97-157.

Taylor, R. M. S., 1962. Non-metrical Studies in the Human Palate and Dentition in Maori and Moriori Skulls. Parts I and II. *Journal of the Polynesian Society*. Vol. 71, pp. 8-100 and 167-187.

Disease

Brothwell, D. (Ed.), 1967. *Diseases in Antiquity*. Thomas, Springfield.

Houghton, P., 1975. A Renal Calculus from Protohistoric New Zealand. *Ossa*. Vol. 2, pp. 11-14.

Houghton, P., 1977. Trephination in Oceania. *Journal of the Polynesian Society*. Vol. 86, pp. 265-269.

A small number of skeletal reports have been published:

Houghton, P., 1975. The People of Wairau Bar. *Records of the Canterbury Museum*. Vol. 9, pp. 231-246.

Houghton, P., 1975. Report on the Teviotdale Skeletal Material. In Prehistoric Burials at Teviotdale, North Canterbury, by M. M. Trotter. *Records of the Canterbury Museum*. Vol. 9, pp. 221-230.

Houghton, P., 1977. Prehistoric Burials from Recent Excavations on Motutapu Island. *Records of the Auckland Institute and Museum*. Vol. 14, pp. 37-43.

Houghton, P., 1977. Human Skeletal Material from Excavations in Eastern Coromandel. *Records of the Auckland Institute and Museum*. Vol. 14, pp. 45-46.

Index

Micronesia

Solomons

Melanesia

New Hebrides

Fiji

New Caledonia

Ellice

New Ze

Ch

Motutapu
Island

Opito

Castlepoint

Wairau Bar

Kaikoura